Key Stage 3

Maths

Summary and Practice Book

Name ....

School ....

Class / Set ....

Stanley Thornes (Publishers) Ltd

How to use this book

This book has been carefully designed to help you to prepare for the National Key Stage 3 Tests that all students do in Year 9.

You will take the Tests at one of four 'tiers'; Tier 3–5, Tier 4–6, Tier 5–7 or Tier 6–8. The numbers in these tiers are the National Curriculum levels. They are an indication of the difficulty of the work.

This book will help you to revise and give you practice for all of the tiers. You need to know which tier you are aiming for before you start using the book.

The book covers the National Curriculum in 13 short clear topics. On the opposite page, you can see how the book has been designed to help you study and practise your Maths. You should read this carefully before you start to use the book.

There are lots of Practice Questions. These are like the questions that you will get on the Maths Tests. One of the best ways to revise Maths is to do lots of practice questions and check your answers.

When answering the questions you can write your answers in the spaces or write them on a sheet of paper. Your teacher will tell you which method to use.

The answers to the Test Yourself tests are given at the back of the book. Your teacher will have the answers to the Practice Questions if they are not at the back of your version of the book.

Don't just copy the answers out. That won't help you learn! Try the questions and then check your answers. You can learn a lot by checking your own answers and looking to see where you may have lost marks, so that you can do better next time.

We hope you will find this book very helpful in preparing yourself for the Tests.

Paul Hogan
Barbara Job

There are 13 topics in this book. Each one starts with work that **everyone needs to know**.

If you are doing Tier 6–8 or Tier 5–7 you may feel that you don't need to do any of the early part of each chapter. It is still a good idea to read it and do the Test Yourself and Practice Questions to make sure that you understand everything!

1 Each chapter is clearly labelled.

2 A picture sets the scene.

3 The first section covers Levels 3–5. **This is all you need to do if you're doing Tier 3–5.**

4 Then there may be a Level 6 section. You only need to do this if you're doing Level 6.

5 Now Test Yourself on Levels 3–5.

6 … and Level 6 if you need to …

7 … and do the Practice Questions for Levels 3–5 and Level 6 if you need to.

8 Now do the Level 7 section if you need to …

9 … and the Level 8 section. You only need to do this if you're doing Tier 6–8.

10 Now Test Yourself on Level 7 …

11 and Level 8 if you need to …

12 … and do the Practice Questions for Levels 5–7 …

13 and Level 8 if you need to.

Contents

Shape, space and measures

Handling data

1 Whole numbers

The Celsius scale has the freezing point of water at 0 °C.
Temperatures below 0 °C have minus signs in front.
The temperature in this freezer is −10 °C.

Levels 3–5

- You need to know your tables up to the 10 times table.

- The position of a digit in a number is important.
  The 7 in 571 is worth 7 tens = 70
  The 7 in 4760 is worth 7 hundreds = 700

Th	H	T	U
	5	7	1
4	7	6	0

- When you multiply by 10 all the digits move one column to the left.
  The number gets bigger.

H	T	U
	4	6
4	6	0

  $46 \times 10 = 460$

- When you divide by 10 all the digits move one column to the right.
  The number gets smaller.

H	T	U
5	8	0
	5	8

  $580 \div 10 = 58$

- When you multiply or divide by 100 the digits move two columns instead of one.

- When you multiply or divide by 1000 the digits move three columns.

Th	H	T	U
2	3	0	0
		2	3

  $2300 \div 100 = 23$

- Addition and subtraction without a calculator
  Put the digits in the correct columns.
  In this question $8 + 5 = 13$
  Put the 3 in the units column and carry the 1.

H	T	U
	2	4	8
+		2	5
	2	7	3

- You may have to borrow in subtractions.
  You cannot take 9 from 6. You borrow a ten to give
  $16 - 9 = 7$

H	T	U
2	²3̸	¹6
−		1	9
	2	1	7

- **Multiplication without a calculator**
  Multiply by the units digit first.
  Put 0 in the units column before multiplying
  by the tens digit.
  Add the two parts.

$$
\begin{array}{r}
1\ 2\ 3 \\
\times\ \ \ 3\ 2 \\
\hline
2\ 4\ 6 \\
3\ 6\ 9\ 0 \\
\hline
3\ 9\ 3\ 6 \\
\scriptstyle 1
\end{array}
$$

- **Division without a calculator**
  In this question start by working out the
  13 times table.
  $31 \div 13 = 2$ with 5 to carry because
  $2 \times 13 = 26$ and $31 - 26 = 5$
  Then $52 \div 13 = 4$ because $4 \times 13 = 52$

$$
\begin{array}{r}
2\ 4 \\
13\,\overline{)3\ 1\ {}^{5}2}
\end{array}
$$

$1 \times 13 = 13$
$2 \times 13 = 26$
$3 \times 13 = 39$
$4 \times 13 = 52$

- **Negative numbers have a minus sign in front of them.**
  This thermometer shows a temperature of $-5\,°C$
  $-10\,°C$ is lower than $-5\,°C$.
     $5\,°C$ is higher than $-5\,°C$.

- **Use a thermometer scale to help you add and subtract.**
  To work out $-5 + 8$ start at -5 and move up 8.
  You get to 3   so $-5 + 8 = 3$
  To work out $-5 - 2$ start at -5 and move down 2.
  You get to -7 so $-5 - 2 = -7$

Level 6

- **Adding and subtracting with negative numbers.**
  $6 - -3 = 6 + 3 = 9$ $--$ becomes $+$
  $7 + -2 = 7 - 2 = 5$ $+-$ becomes $-$
  $-4 - -5 = -4 + 5 = 1$
  $-2 + -6 = -2 - 6 = -8$

- **Multiplying and dividing with negative numbers.**
  $+ \times + = +$ $- \times - = +$ Two signs the same give $+$
  $+ \times - = -$ $- \times + = -$ Two different signs give $-$
  The same rules work for division.
  $+4 \times +3 = +12$ $-4 \times -6 = +24$ $+12 \div +6 = +2$ $-24 \div -6 = +4$
  $+5 \times -2 = -10$ $-10 \times +3 = -30$ $+20 \div -5 = -4$ $-16 \div +2 = -8$

Levels 3–5

1 The value of

	Th	H	T	U
	5	1	3	8

  a the 3 is ......

  b the 1 is ......

2 **a** $4 \times 7 =$ ......   **b** $6 \times 9 =$ ......   **c** $8 \times$ ...... $= 24$

3 **a** $26 \times 10 =$ ......   **b** $41 \times 100 =$ ......   **c** $53 \times$ ...... $= 530$

4 **a** $360 \div 10 =$ ......   **b** $8000 \div 100 =$ ......   **c** $4860 \div$ ...... $= 486$

5 **a** $\begin{array}{r} 260 \\ + 123 \\ \hline \end{array}$ **b** $\begin{array}{r} 187 \\ + 35 \\ \hline \end{array}$ **c** $\begin{array}{r} 174 \\ - 51 \\ \hline \end{array}$ **d** $\begin{array}{r} 271 \\ - 46 \\ \hline \end{array}$

6 **a** $\begin{array}{r} 237 \\ \times\ 25 \\ \hline \\ \hline \end{array}$ **b** $14\overline{)322}$ $1 \times 14 =$
        $2 \times 14 =$
        $3 \times 14 =$

7 Put these numbers in order $12, -4, -6, 5, 0$

  Start with the smallest   ...... , ... , ... , ... , ...

8 The temperature is $-2\,°C$. It rises $5\,°C$. The new temperature is ...... $°C$.

Level 6

9 **a** $4 - -6 =$ ......   **d** $20 \div -4 =$ ......   **g** $-5 \times$ ...... $= 15$

  b $-8 - 3 =$ ......   **e** $18 - -2 =$ ......   **h** $-36 \div$ ...... $= -6$

  c $-4 \times -7 =$ ......   **f** $-6 + -12 =$ ......   **i** ...... $\div -10 = -5$

Levels 3–5

1 Here are some number cards.

| 4 | 2 | 3 | 5 |

    a Write down the **smallest** number that can be made with these cards.

                      .... 1 mark

    b Write down the **largest** number that can be made with these cards.

                      .... 1 mark

    c Which extra card is needed to make a number **ten** times bigger than **4235**?

                      .... 1 mark

2 a A shop sells CDs for **£13** each.
    Find the cost of **25 CDs**.
    Show your working.

Cost of 25 CDs is £ .... 2 marks

    b The shop also sells packs of video tapes for **£18**.
    What is the greatest number of packs of video tapes that could be bought
    with **£300**?
    Show your working.

.... packs   2 marks

3 a Write down the **temperature** shown by the arrow.

.... °C   1 mark

b Draw an arrow on the scale to show a temperature of **8 °C**.

1 mark

c A temperature of **4 °C** went down **6 °C**.
What is the temperature now?

.... °C   1 mark

Level 6

---

4 −5, −4, −3, −2, −1, 0, 1, 2, 3, 4, 5

Choose a number from the list above which will give

a the **lowest** possible answer

−4 − .... = ...   1 mark

b the **highest** possible answer

−4 − .... = ...   1 mark

In each case also work out the answer.

5 Substitute the values $a = 15$, $b = -2$ into the formula and work out the value of T:

$$T = \frac{4a}{b}$$

T = ...   1 mark

- **When you multiply by a number between 0 and 1 the answer will be smaller than the number you started with.**

  $200 \times 0.5 = 100$ 100 is less than 200
  $300 \times \frac{2}{3} = 200$ 200 is less than 300

- **When you divide by a number between 0 and 1 the answer will be larger than the number you started with.**

  $200 \div 0.5 = 400$ 400 is more than 200
  $300 \div \frac{2}{3} = 450$ 450 is more than 300

- **Use the bracket keys [( )] on your calculator to help you work out complicated problems.**

  To work out $\dfrac{246 - 157}{4.3 \times 9.1}$ put brackets around the top and bottom. Key in

  [(] [2] [4] [6] [−] [1] [5] [7] [)] [÷] [(] [4] [.] [3] [×] [9] [.] [1] [)] [=]

  to get 2.27 to 2 dp.

- 5^3 means $5 \times 5 \times 5$. The power 3 tells you how many 5s to multiply together.

- **A power of 2 is called square.**
  10^2 means 10×10
  You say this as 'ten squared'.

- **A power of 3 is called cube.**
  10^3 means $10 \times 10 \times 10$
  You say this as 'ten cubed'.

- **The opposite of 'square' is 'square root'.**
  $\sqrt{25} = 5$ because $5 \times 5 = 25$

- **The opposite of 'cube' is 'cube root'.**
  You write the cube root as $\sqrt[3]{}$
  $\sqrt[3]{8} = 2$ because $2 \times 2 \times 2 = 8$

- **Any number can be written as a number between 1 and 10 multiplied by a power of 10.** This is called standard form. To write 67 000 in standard form, the number between 1 and 10 is 6.7. You need to multiply 6.7 by 10 four times to get 67 000.

So 67 000 = 6.7 × 10⁴

$$6.\overset{1\ 2\ 3\ 4}{7\,0\,0\,0}.$$

To write 0.000 024 6 in standard form, the number between 1 and 10 is 2.46 You need to divide by 10 five times to get to 0.000 024 6.

To show you have to divide, put a minus sign in the power.

$$0.\overset{5\ 4\ 3\ 2\ 1}{0\,0\,0\,0\,2}.4\,6$$

So 0.000 024 6 = 2.46 × 10⁻⁵

- **You use these rules to change numbers in standard form back to ordinary numbers.**

7.13 × 10⁶ = 7 130 000

$$7.\overset{1\ 2\ 3\ 4\ 5\ 6}{1\,3\,0\,0\,0\,0}.$$

4.02 × 10⁻³ = 0.004 02

$$0.\overset{3\ 2\ 1}{0\,0}4.0\,2$$

- Most calculators have an **EXP** or **EE** key. You can use this key to enter numbers in standard form.

For 7.13 × 10⁶ key in **7** **.** **1** **3** **EXP** **6**

The calculator display will look like 7.13^{06}

Use the **+/−** key to enter negative powers.

For 4.02 × 10⁻³ key in **4** **.** **0** **2** **EXP** **3** **+/−**

The calculator display will look like 4.02^{-03}

- **Never write the calculator display as your answer.**

6.5^{-04} must be written 6.5 × 10⁻⁴.

To work out 3.9 × 10⁴ ÷ 1.3 × 10⁻⁶ key in

3 **.** **9** **EXP** **4** **÷** **1** **.** **3** **EXP** **6** **+/−** **=**

to get $3.^{10}$. You must write this as 3 × 10¹⁰.

TEST YOURSELF

Level 7

1 Fill in the space with $\times$ or $\div$

  a 36 ...... 0.12 = 300   **c** 260 ...... 0.4 = 104

  b 50 ...... 0.3 = 15   **d** 150 ...... 0.1 = 1500

2 Write down the calculator keys you would press to work out

  a $\dfrac{4.86 \times 1.63}{4.37 + 1.94}$ ....

  ....

  b $\dfrac{4.2 + 3.6^2}{4.91 - 2.87}$ ....

  ....

Level 8

3 **a** $25^2 =$ ....   **c** $\sqrt[3]{27} =$ ....

  b the square root of 81 is ......   **d** the cube root of ...... is 4

4 Write these numbers in standard form

  a 0.005 = ...   **b** 12 million = ...

5 Write these as ordinary numbers

  a $2.81 \times 10^5 =$ ....   **b** $8.3 \times 10^{-7} =$ ....

6 Write down the calculator keys you would press to work out

  $4.2 \times 10^6 \div 2.1 \times 10^{-4}$ ....

  ....

13

Levels 5–7

1 Write numbers into each of the empty boxes so that each problem will work out correctly.

a $\boxed{821} - \boxed{647} = \boxed{}$

d $\boxed{182} \div \boxed{7} = \boxed{}$

b $\boxed{} \times \boxed{} \times \boxed{5} = \boxed{40}$

e $\boxed{} - \boxed{} = \boxed{31}$

c $\boxed{1400} \div \boxed{} = \boxed{14}$

f $\boxed{37} \times \boxed{9} = \boxed{}$

6 marks

2 Sean makes large wax candles that are sold for £27 each.

a Sean sells **34** candles.
How much does he get for the **34** candles?
Show all your working clearly.

£ .... 2 marks

b Sean packs **12** candles in a box.
He has **200** candles.
How many full boxes can he pack with the **200** candles?
Show all your working.

.... boxes   2 marks

3 $K = \dfrac{14.2p}{q - r}$

Use your calculator to find K when $p = 37.4$, $q = 80.4$, $r = 13.53$

$K = $ ....   1 mark

4 The table shows information about the local taxes raised in four towns.

Town	Taxes	Population
A	£86 850 000	347 400
B	£119 945 000	521 500
C	£98 784 000	403 200
D	£170 977 500	670 500

    a Which town had the lowest tax per person? .... 1 mark

    b Which town had the highest tax per person? .... 1 mark

Level 8

5 Light travels at the speed of 9.46×10^{12} km/year.

    The time it takes for light to reach Earth from the edge of the known universe is 15 000 000 000 years.

    a Write the number 15 000 000 000 in standard form.

    .... 1 mark

    b Calculate the distance in kilometres from the edge of the known universe to Earth. Give your answer in standard form.

    .... 2 marks

6 In the United States a centillion is 10^{303}.
    In the United Kingdom a centillion is 10^{600}.
    How many times bigger is a United Kingdom centillion than a United States centillion?

    .... 2 marks

2 Fractions, decimals and percentages

You would never see a price like this!

Levels 3–5

- **An amount of money which has both pounds and pence must have 2 decimal places.**
  £6.43 is £6 and 43 pence.

- **Your calculator sometimes only gives 1 decimal place.**
  If you work out £30 ÷ 4 on your calculator
  your display will look like this
  You must write the answer as £7.50

  7.5

- **The position of a digit after a decimal point is important.**
  The value of the 3 is 3 tenths or $\frac{3}{10}$.
  The value of the 8 is 8 hundredths or $\frac{8}{100}$.

U	t	h
4 .	3	8

- **Adding and subtracting decimals without a calculator.**
  Put the digits in the correct columns.
  In this question 7 + 6 = 13
  Put the 3 in the 't' column and carry the 1.

  ```
  T U . t h
  3 5 . 7 4
  + 1 2 . 6
  ---------
  4 8 . 3 4
        1
  ```

- **You may have to borrow in subtractions.**
  You cannot take 8 from 2 in the 't' column.
  You borrow one from the 'U' column to give 12 − 8 = 4

  ```
  T U . t h
  3 4⁄5 . ¹2 7
  − 1 3 . 8 5
  ----------
  2 1 . 4 2
  ```

- **Always make sure the decimal points go underneath each other.**

- **When you multiply by 10 all the digits move one column to the left.**
  The number gets bigger.

$$3.56 \times 10 = 35.6$$

- **When you divide by 10 all the digits move one column to the right.**
  The number gets smaller.

$$6.8 \div 10 = 0.68$$

- **When you multiply or divide by 100 the digits move two columns instead of one.**

$$596 \div 100 = 5.96$$

- **When you multiply or divide by 1000 the digits move three columns.**

$$0.51 \times 1000 = 510$$

- **Multiplying decimals without a calculator.**
  Start with the 4.
  The $_2$ and the $_1$ are carries.
  Put 0 in the right hand column before multiplying by the 2
  The $_1$ is a carry.
  Now add the two parts together.
  Make sure you don't add the carries.

$$
\begin{array}{r}
1\,2\,.\,6\,3 \\
\times \quad\quad 2\,4 \\
\hline
5\,_2 0\,.\,_1 5\,2 \\
2\,_1 5\,2\,.\,6\,0 \\
\hline
3\,0\,3\,.\,1\,2
\end{array}
$$

- **Dividing decimals without a calculator.**
  $7 \div 5 = 1$ with 2 to carry
  $24 \div 5 = 4$ with 4 to carry
  $41 \div 5 = 8$ with 1 to carry
  Add a zero
  $10 \div 5 = 2$

$$
\begin{array}{r}
1\,4\,.\,8\,2 \\
5\overline{)7^2 4\,.\,^4 1^1 0}
\end{array}
$$

- **To write down the fraction shaded.**
  Count the number of shaded sections.
  This number goes on the top of the fraction.

  Count the total number of equal sections.
  This number goes on the bottom of the fraction.

$$\frac{5}{9}$$

- **Different fractions can show the same amount.**

$$\frac{1}{4} \quad = \quad \frac{2}{8}$$

$\frac{1}{4}$ and $\frac{2}{8}$ are equivalent fractions

- **To find a fraction of an amount multiply by the top number and divide by the bottom number.**

  So $\frac{3}{5}$ of 400 g = 240 g

  $400 \times 3 = 1200$
  $1200 \div 5 = 240$

- **A percentage is a fraction where the bottom number is 100.**
  This circle has 100 equal sections.
  There are 15 shaded sections.

  The fraction shaded is $\frac{15}{100}$

  This is the same as 15%

- $\frac{1}{10} = 10\%$ $\frac{1}{5} = 20\%$ $\frac{1}{4} = 25\%$ $\frac{1}{2} = 50\%$

  $\frac{7}{10} = 70\%$ $\frac{2}{5} = 40\%$ $\frac{3}{4} = 75\%$

- **To find a percentage of an amount multiply by the percentage and divide by 100.**

  So 65% of £800 = £520

  $800 \times 65 = 52\,000$
  $52\,000 \div 100 = 520$

- **To put decimals in order of size.**
  Look at the number before the decimal point first.

    26.415 is smaller than 40.1 because 26 is smaller than 40

  If the numbers before the decimal point are the same, look at the first number after the decimal point.

    6.372 is smaller than 6.43 because 3 is smaller than 4

  Sometimes you need to look at the second number after the decimal point.

    7.208 is smaller than 7.261 because 0 is smaller than 6

  Carry on like this. Look at one decimal place at a time.

- **To change a fraction to a decimal divide the top number by the bottom number.**

  $$\frac{7}{8} = 7 \div 8 = 0.875$$

- **To change a percentage to a fraction put it over 100.** Then you can get to a decimal by dividing if you need to.

  $$23\% = \frac{23}{100} = 0.23$$

- **To put a mixture of fractions, percentages and decimals in order, change them all to decimals first.**
  Remember to change them back at the end.

- **To change a decimal to a percentage multiply it by 100. To turn this into a fraction put it over 100.**

  $$0.31 = 0.31 \times 100\%$$
  $$= 31\%$$

  $$0.31 = 31\% = \frac{31}{100}$$

- You should be able to use the $a\frac{b}{c}$ key on your calculator to help you do fractions.

- **To write one number as a fraction of another number.**
  Make sure the units are the same.
  Put the first number on top of the second number.

  Use the $a\frac{b}{c}$ key to see if your fraction will cancel.

  To write 45 as a fraction of 180.

  Start with $\frac{45}{180}$. Key in [4] [5] [$a\frac{b}{c}$] [1] [8] [0] [=]

  to get $\frac{1}{4}$ which is the simplest form of the fraction.

- **To write one number as a percentage of another number.**

  Write the numbers as a fraction.
  Change the fraction to a percentage by multiplying by 100.
  To write 26 as a percentage of 40

  Start with $\dfrac{26}{40} = \dfrac{26}{40} \times 100\% = 65\%$

- **Ratio can be used to compare two quantities.**

  There are 2 red counters
  and 4 blue counters

  The ratio   red : blue
       is   2 : 4

  You can simplify this because 2 goes into both numbers
  red : blue = 1 : 2

- **Ratio can also be used to show how a quantity is divided up.**

  To divide £70 in the ratio 2 : 3

  Find the total number of parts by
  adding the numbers in the ratio.   2 + 3 = 5 parts

  Find the value of one part.   £70 ÷ 5 = £14
  Work out the value of each share.   £14 × 2 = £28
                                            £14 × 3 = £42

- **Scales on maps are often given as a ratio of the form 1 : n**

  Any ratio can be changed to this form.
  Divide both of the numbers in the ratio by the first number

  $$2 : 3 = \frac{2}{2} : \frac{3}{2} = 1 : 1.5$$

- **Sometimes ratios are given in the form n : 1**

  This time divide both numbers by the second number

  $$3 : 8 = \frac{3}{8} : \frac{8}{8} = 0.375 : 1$$

Levels 3–5

1 a   2.14   **b**   12.76   **c**   2.53   **d**
    + 1.79   − 8.58   × _24_   5)8.95
    ‾‾‾‾   ‾‾‾‾‾   ‾‾‾‾‾

2 a $\frac{5}{8}$ of £224 = £ ....   **b** 72% of 900 g = ... g

       ...... ÷ ...... = ... ÷ ...... = ...

       ...... × ...... = ... × ...... = ...

3 a Colour in 25%   **b** Colour in $\frac{3}{4}$

Level 6

4

Fraction	$\frac{1}{2}$	......	......	$\frac{3}{4}$	......	......
Decimal	......	0.25	......	......	0.6	......
Percentage	......	......	20%	......	......	81%

5 a 16 as a fraction of 40   **b** 35p as a percentage of £2.50

      is $\dfrac{......}{......} = \dfrac{......}{......}$ = 35p as a percentage of ......p = $\dfrac{......}{......} \times 100\%$

                                                                      = ...%

6 Share £180 in the ratio 2 : 3 : 4

    Total number of parts = ...

    Value of 1 part = ... ÷ ...... = £ ......

    Value of each share

    2 × ...... = £......   ...... × ...... = £......   ...... × ...... = £......

1 Kathy and Neil each have 16 counters.

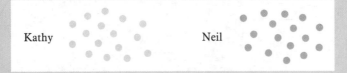

   a Kathy uses **half** her counters for a game.
      How many counters does Kathy use?

                                                                  .... 1 mark

   b Neil uses **4** counters for his game.
      What **fraction** of his counters did Neil use?

                                                                  .... 1 mark

   c How many counters does Kathy have left?

                                                                  .... 1 mark

   d How many counters does Neil have left?

                                                                  .... 1 mark

2 Here are the ingredients for a Greek meal.
The table shows the quantities needed for 6 people.

6 people	9 people
Cloves of garlic: 2	Cloves of garlic: ......
Chick peas: 4 ounces	Chick peas: ...... ounces
Tablespoons olive oil: 4	Tablespoons olive oil: ......
Paste: 5 fluid ounces	Paste: ...... fluid ounces

Complete the table to show the quantities needed for 9 people.   2 marks

3 **a** What **fraction** of the diagram is shaded?

.... 1 mark

b What **percentage** of the diagram is shaded?

.... 1 mark

c Shade $\frac{2}{3}$ of the second diagram.

1 mark

4 Kevin has bought a computer game from his uncle.
His uncle asks him for weekly payments which are either **5% of £30** or $\frac{2}{5}$ **of £4**.

a Work out 5% of £30.   £ .... 1 mark

b Work out $\frac{2}{5}$ of £4.   £ .... 1 mark

c Which is the least amount that Kevin
will need to pay per week?   £ .... 1 mark

Level 6

5 To make a shade of orange paint, **2 parts red** is mixed with **3 parts yellow**.
12 litres of **yellow** paint are to be mixed with red paint to make some orange paint.

a How many litres of **red** paint are needed?

.... litres of red paint   2 marks

b What is the total quantity of **orange** paint made?

.... litres of orange paint   1 mark

- **To increase an amount by a given fraction or percentage.**
  Work out the fraction or percentage.
  Add it on to the amount you started with.

  Increase £400 by 5%   5% of £400 = £20
                         New amount = £420

- **To decrease an amount by a given fraction or percentage.**
  Work out the fraction or percentage.
  Take it away from the amount you started with.

  Reduce 375 g by $\frac{2}{15}$ $\frac{2}{15}$ of 375 g = 50 g
                                    New amount = 325 g

- **You may have to increase or decrease the amount more than once.**
  £100 is invested. Each year 6% is added as interest.
  Find the balance after 3 years.

Year 1	Interest = 6% of £100 = £6	New balance = £106
Year 2	Interest = 6% of £106 = £6.36	New balance = £112.36
Year 3	Interest = 6% of £112.36 = £6.74	New balance = £119.10

- **You may be given the final amount and how it has been changed. You will have to find the original amount.**
  A coat is reduced by 15% in a sale. The sale price is £61.20
  Find the original price.
  The sale price is 100% − 15% = 85% of the original price.
  So 1% of the original price = £61.20 ÷ 85 = £0.72
  100% of the original price = £0.72 × 100 = £72

- **Sometimes changes are given as fractions**
  $\frac{5}{12}$ of a number is 45.
  Find the number.
  $\frac{5}{12}$ is 45 so $\frac{1}{12}$ is 45 ÷ 5 = 9.
  So $\frac{12}{12}$ = 9 × 12 = 108

Level 7

1 Increase **a** 650 g by 20%   **b** £460 by $\frac{2}{5}$

    a 20% of ...... = ...   **b** ...... of ...... = ...

    New amount = ... g   New amount = £ ......

2 Decrease **a** 370 cm by 15%   **b** 2400 kg by $\frac{3}{8}$

    a ...... of ...... = ... cm   **b** ...... of ...... = ... kg

    New amount = ... cm   New amount = ... kg

3 VAT at 17.5% is added to a bill of £60. Find the total.

    17.5% of ...... = £ ......   Total bill = £ ......

Level 8

4 Asha buys a car for £8600. The value of the car decreases by 15% every year. How much is the car worth after 3 years?

    Year 1 Loss = 15% of ...... = £ ......   New value = £ ......

    Year 2 Loss = ... of ...... = £ ......   New value = £ ......

    Year 3 Loss = ... of ...... = £ ......   New value = £ ......

5 The population of Plumley village has increased by 7% since 1990. It is now 2568. What was the population in 1990?

New population = 100% + ... = ... % of the 1990 population

So 1% of 1990 population = ... ÷ ...... = ...

100% of 1990 population = ... × 100 = ...

6 Every year a firm increases its workforce by $\frac{3}{17}$.
This year the firm will take on 420 people.
How many people work for the firm at the moment.

$\frac{3}{17}$ is ...... so $\frac{......}{......}$ is .... Number of people now is ...... × ...... = ...

1 Complete these calculations.

    a .... $\times 150 = 54$

    b $5.4 \div$ .... $= 54$

    c $675 \times$ .... $= 54$ 3 marks

2 A cake is divided into four pieces.

    The first three pieces are: $\frac{1}{2}$ of the cake

                                $\frac{1}{4}$ of the cake

                                $\frac{1}{8}$ of the cake

    a What **fraction** of the cake is the fourth piece?   .... 1 mark

    b Each $\frac{1}{16}$ of the cake has a mass of **20 g**.
        What is the mass of the piece which is $\frac{1}{4}$ of the cake? .... g 2 marks

3 There are **295** pupils in Year 8 and Year 9 at a school.

	Year 8	Year 9
Boys	60	90
Girls	75	70

    a What **percentage** of these pupils are in **Year 9**?   ....% 2 marks

    b Write the **ratio** of boys to girls in the form 1 : n

                                    Ratio of boys to girls is 1 : ...... 2 marks

4 Simon keeps $\frac{3}{8}$ of his money in his piggy bank and spends the rest.

   a What **fraction** of his money does he spend? .... 1 mark

   b What **percentage** of his money does he spend? .... % 1 mark

   c He has £24 to start with.
      How much does he **save**? £ .... 1 mark

Level 8

5 The value of a computer is expected to fall by 20% every year.

   a What is the value of a computer which is 2 years old,
      if it had a value of £800 when new?

      £ .... 2 marks

   b A different computer has a value of £704
      when it is 2 years old.
      What was its value when it was new? £ .... 2 marks

   c What single decimal number could you multiply
      the original value of a computer by, to find its value

      (i) after 2 years? ....

      (ii) after n years? .... 2 marks

   d A new computer is advertised with a price of £1500.
      What will its value be after 4 years?

      £ .... 2 marks

   e How many years will it take for the value of
      any computer to fall by more than half of its
      original value .... years 2 marks

3   Estimating

'When I said put brackets on your calculator ...'

Levels 3–5

- **BODMAS**
  This tells you which parts of a number question to do first.

First do	Brackets
then powers	**O**f
Next do	**D**ivision
and	**M**ultiplication
Then	**A**ddition
and	**S**ubtraction

  $4 + 3 \times 7$
  $= 4 + 21$ BOD**MA**S
  $= 25$ $\times$ before $+$

  $16 \div (2 + 6)$ Bo**D**MAS
  $= 16 \div 8$ ( ) before $\div$
  $= 2$

- **Rounding to the nearest whole number**
  Round 7.6 to the nearest whole number.

  7.6 is nearer to 8 than to 7.
  It is rounded to 8 to the nearest whole number.

- **Rounding to the nearest 10**
  Round 263 to the nearest 10.

  263 is nearer to 260 than to 270. It is rounded to 260 to the nearest 10.

- **Rounding to the nearest 100**
  Round 750 to the nearest 100.

  750 is half way between 700 and 800. It is rounded to 800 to the nearest 100.

- **When you use a calculator check that your answer is about the right size.**
  It is very easy to hit the wrong key!

  Work out 3.6 × 239   **3** . **6** × **2** **3** **9** =   Answer = *860.4*

  Estimate: 3.6 is 4 to the nearest whole number.
  239 is 200 to the nearest 100.
  4 × 200 = 800
  800 is near to 860.4 so the answer is probably right.

- **You can also check your answer by writing a new problem.**
  226 × 13 = 2938
  To check this you can work out
  either   2938 ÷ 13   or   2938 ÷ 226
  to get 226   to get 13

Level 6

- **You also need to be able to round decimal numbers.**
  Round 3.14 to 1 decimal place

  3.14 is closer to 3.1 than to 3.2
  It is rounded to 3.1 to 1 decimal place (1 dp)

  Round 2.568 to 2 decimal places.

  2.568 is closer to 2.57 than to 2.56
  It is rounded to 2.57 to 2 decimal places (2 dp)

- **You can use this rule of rounding instead of drawing scales.**
  Look at the first unwanted digit. If it is 5, 6, 7, 8 or 9 add one to the last digit you
  want to keep. If the first 'unwanted' digit is 0, 1, 2, 3, 4, you do not add one.

  5.38 is 5.4 to 1 dp   12.5731 is 12.57 to 2 dp.

TEST YOURSELF

1 Use BODMAS to work out

  a $15 + 12 \div 4$ **c** $3 \times 8 - 4$ **e** $(8 + 6) \div 2 + 7$

     = ... + ...   = ... − ......   = ...

     = ...   = ...   = ... = ...

  b $26 - 3 \times 5$ **d** $7 \times (12 - 8)$ **f** $3^2 + 4 \times 6$

     = ... − ......   = ...   = ...

     = ...   = ...   = ...

2 **a** 2.3 = ... to the nearest whole number   **d** 434 = ... to the nearest 100

  b 46 = ... to the nearest 10   **e** 99 = ... to the nearest 10

  c 137 = ... to the nearest 10

3 **a** 34×176 = ...   **b** $858 \div 33$ = ...

   Estimate: Estimate:

    34 = ... to the nearest 10   858 = ... to the nearest 100

    176 = ... to the nearest 100   33 = ... to the nearest 10

    ...... × ...... = ... ÷ ...... = ...

Level 6

4 **a** 7.85 = ... to 1 dp   **d** 29.086 = ... to 2 dp

  b 6.3174 = ... to 2 dp   **e** 4.857 31 = ... to 3 dp

  c 13.418 = ... to 1 dp   **f** 4.6954 = ... to 2 dp

5 A box of 8 tapes costs £11.50
Find the cost of 1 tape.

1 tape costs £...... ÷ ...... = £...... to the nearest penny

1 The attendance at a football match was **346 487**.
A local newspaper wants to print the attendance figure.
Write down a **sensible** number for them to use. .... 1 mark

2 Complete the problems.

a .... ÷ .... = 5

b You may use the signs +, −, ×, ÷

24 ...... 3 ...... 1 = 9 2 marks

3 The table shows the number of pupils in four neighbouring schools.

School	Number of pupils	To the nearest 100	To the nearest 10
Olney	884		
Mesnes	662		
Heaton	788		
Pendle	906		

4 marks

a Complete the table to show the number of pupils rounded to the nearest **100** pupils, and to the nearest **10** pupils.
b Salus School has **700** pupils, to the nearest **100** pupils, and **650** pupils, to the nearest **10** pupils.
Write down two possible figures for the number of pupils.

.... and .... 2 marks

4 Anita has worked out some questions.
For each question write down another problem she could do to check accurately the answer she has worked out.

a 359 × 13 = 4667 Check: .... 1 mark

b 377 + 761 = 1138 Check: .... 1 mark

c 1830 − 727 = 1103 Check: .... 1 mark

d 5287 ÷ 17 = 311 Check: .... 1 mark

- **The first significant figure in any number is the first digit which isn't a 0.**
  For most numbers this is the first digit.
  The first significant figure in these numbers is the red digit

      257   81.5   0.621   0.000 316   0.020 31

- **Rounding to 1 significant figure (1 sf)**
  Look at the digit after the first significant one   0.064
  Use the rule of rounding.   0.06

- **Be careful to keep the number about the right size.**

      738 is 700 to 1 sf.   It is not 7
      4629 is 5000 to 1 sf.   It is not 5

- **When numbers are given to 1 sf they are easy to multiply and divide.**

  $400 \times 2000 = 800\,000$ $4 \times 100 \times 2 \times 1000$
  $\qquad\qquad\qquad\qquad\qquad\qquad = 8 \times 100\,000$

  $0.03 \times 0.2 = 0.006$ $3 \div 100 \times 2 \div 10$
  $\qquad\qquad\qquad\qquad\qquad\qquad = 6 \div 1000$

  $0.003 \times 70 = 0.21$ $3 \div 1000 \times 7 \times 10$
  $\qquad\qquad\qquad\qquad\qquad\qquad = 21 \div 100$

  $8000 \div 20 = 400$ $\dfrac{^{4}\cancel{8} \times 100\cancel{0}}{\cancel{2} \times \cancel{10}} = 4 \times 100$

  $600 \div 0.3 = 2000$ $600 \div \dfrac{3}{10} = {}^{2}\cancel{6}00 \times \dfrac{10}{\cancel{3}}$

- **Estimating square roots**
  Round the number to the nearest square number

      $\sqrt{39} \simeq \sqrt{36} = 6$

  If you round $\sqrt{39}$ to 1 sf you get $\sqrt{40}$. You still can't do this in your head.

  The square numbers are   1,   4,   9,   16,   25,   ...
                            1×1 2×2 3×3 4×4 5×5

Level 7

1 Round these to 1 sf.

   a $3.94 = $ ......

   b $0.0718 = $ ......

   c $26 = $ ......

   d $0.007\,006 = $ ......

   e $6503 = $ ......

   f $9500 = $ ......

2 **a** $500 \times 1000 = $ ......

   b $60 \times 400 = $ ......

   c $0.003 \times 0.1 = $ ......

   d $0.06 \times 0.007 = $ ......

   e $0.2 \times 400 = $ ......

   f $0.03 \times 5000 = $ ......

   g $9000 \div 30 = $ ......

   h $1000 \div 50 = $ ......

   i $700 \div 0.1 = $ ......

   j $900 \div 0.03 = $ ......

3 Estimate the value of

   a $\dfrac{41.7 \times 13}{1.56}$

     $= \dfrac{40 \times \text{......}}{\text{......}}$

     $= \dfrac{\text{......}}{\text{......}}$

     $= $ ......

   b $\dfrac{36 \times 44}{13 \times 17}$

     $= \dfrac{\text{......} \times \text{......}}{\text{......} \times \text{......}}$

     $= \dfrac{\text{......}}{\text{......}}$

     $= $ ......

Level 8

4 **a** $\sqrt{17} \simeq \sqrt{\text{......}} = $ ......

   b $\sqrt{87} \simeq \sqrt{\text{......}} = $ ......

5 Estimate the value of $\sqrt{\dfrac{5^2 \times 4^3}{2^4}}$

$$\sqrt{\dfrac{\text{......} \times \text{......}}{\text{......}}} \simeq \sqrt{\dfrac{\text{......} \times \text{......}}{\text{......}}} = \sqrt{\dfrac{\text{......}}{\text{......}}} = \sqrt{\text{......}} \simeq \sqrt{\text{......}} = \text{......}$$

Levels 5–7

1 a A shop sells garden pots for **£2.45**
What is the cost of 4 garden pots?

£ .... 1 mark

b How many garden pots can you buy with **£12**?

.... 1 mark

c The shop also sells the pots in pairs.
One pair of pots costs **£4.49**
How many pairs of pots can you buy with **£12**?

.... pairs 1 mark

d What is the **greatest** number of pots you can buy with **£16**?
You can buy pots either individually or in pairs.

.... pots 1 mark

2 Complete the table below.

Number	Rounded to 1 sf	Rounded to 2 sf	Rounded to 3 sf
0.5182			
10.099			
58.42			
3486			

4 marks

3 Mark wants to work out the calculation

$$\frac{81 \times 155}{42.4 \times 2.4}$$

Find an **estimated** answer to this calculation.
Show all your working.

.... 2 marks

4 A number has been rounded to 3 significant figures.
The result is the answer 5.12

   a Write down the **smallest** number it could have been.

.... 1 mark

   b Write down the **largest** number it could have been.

.... 1 mark

5 Find an **estimated** answer to the expression:

$$\sqrt{\frac{12.2^3 \times 14.3}{440 \times 9.6^2}}$$

.... 2 marks

4 Patterns and sequences

This number pattern is special.
The dots always form a square.

Levels 3–5

- **The square numbers are 1, 4, 9, 16, 25, ...**
  You can draw them as square dot patterns.

  $1 \times 1 = 1$ $2 \times 2 = 4$ $3 \times 3 = 9$ $4 \times 4 = 16$ $5 \times 5 = 25$

- **The triangle numbers are 1, 3, 6, 10, 15, ...**
  You can draw them as triangular dot patterns.

  1 $1 + 2 = 3$ $1 + 2 + 3 = 6$ $1 + 2 + 3 + 4 = 10$ $1 + 2 + 3 + 4 + 5 = 15$

- **The odd numbers are 1, 3, 5, 7, 9, ...**

- **The even numbers are 2, 4, 6, 8, 10, ...**
  These are the numbers in the 2 times table.

- **The multiples of 3 are the 3 times table 3, 6, 9, 12, 15,...**
  The multiples of 5 are the 5 times table 5, 10, 15, 20, 25, ...

- **A number that divides exactly into another number is called a factor.**

  To find the factors of 12
  Look at all the pairs of numbers that
  multiply to give 12
  The factors of 12 are 1, 2, 3, 4, 6, 12

  $12 = 1 \times 12$
  $12 = 2 \times 6$
  $12 = 3 \times 4$

- **Prime numbers have exactly two factors, themselves and 1.**

  $19 = 1 \times 19$ No other two numbers multiply to give 19.
                       So 19 is a prime number.

- **The prime numbers are 2, 3, 5, 7, 11, 13, 17, 19, 23, 29, ...**

  2 is the first prime number. It is the only even prime number.
  1 is not a prime number.

- **The cube numbers are 1, 8, 27, 64, 125, ...**

  $1 \times 1 \times 1 = 1$, $2 \times 2 \times 2 = 8$, $3 \times 3 \times 3 = 27$, $4 \times 4 \times 4 = 64$, $5 \times 5 \times 5 = 125$, ...

- **Square rooting is the opposite of squaring.**

  9 squared $= 9^2 = 9 \times 9 = 81$
  Square root of 81 $= \sqrt{81} = 9$

- **A number sequence is a list of numbers that follows a rule.**
  Each number in a sequence is called a term.

- **To find the rule for a sequence**
  Look at how to get from one term to the next

  The rule for this sequence is **add 4**.
  The 2nd term is $5 + 1$ lot of 4
  The 3rd term is $5 + 2$ lots of 4
  The 20th term is $5 + 19$ lots of 4
  The nth term is $5 + (n - 1)$ lots of 4

Levels 3–5

1 Look at these numbers. Write down

a the multiples of 7 ....

b the prime numbers ....

c the triangle numbers ....

d the cube numbers ....

2 a Write down the first ten multiples of 4.

....

b Write down the first ten multiples of 9.

....

c Write down the number that appears in both lists. ....

3 a 6 squared = ...   **c** Square root of 100 = ...

b 7^2 = ...   **d** $\sqrt{64}$ = ...

Level 6

4 Look at this sequence   3,   8,   13,   18,   23, ...

a The rule is ....

b The 2nd term is 3 + 1 lot of ....

c the 50th term is ...... + ...

d The nth term is ....

Levels 3–5

1   Mrs Kay wants **32** desks in her classroom.
    She can put them in **4** rows,
    with **8** desks in each row.

    a   Draw a diagram to show a **different**
        way that Mrs Kay can arrange the
        32 desks. She must have the same
        number of desks in each row.

        1 mark

    b   Mrs Kay would like to put **6** desks in each row, with the same number of
        desks in each row.
        Explain why Mrs Kay **cannot** arrange the **32** desks in this way.

        .... 1 mark

2   The diagram shows a pattern made out of **black** and **white** tiles.
    The diagram is **6** tiles long.

    a   Continue the diagram so it becomes **10** tiles long.   1 mark
        The table shows the details of the tiles used.

Length of pattern (tiles)	1	2	3	4	5	6
Number of white tiles	3	5	8	10	13	15
Number of black tiles	0	1	1	2	2	3

    The rule for finding the number of white tiles for a length of an
    even number of tiles is

    Number of white tiles = Length $\div\, 2 \times 5$

    b   How many **white tiles** are there in a pattern of length **22 tiles**?

        .... 1 mark

    c   Complete the rule to show the number of **white tiles** for a length of an
        odd number of tiles:

        Number of white tiles = ...   1 mark

3 Melissa arranges some marbles to make a series of patterns.

The number of marbles in each shape is **1, 3, 6**.
To make the next pattern an extra row is added at the bottom.

a Write down the number of marbles in each of the next three patterns.

.... , ... , ...   1 mark

Melissa chooses 5 marbles, but cannot make any shape out of 5 marbles.
She cannot make any shape out of 7 marbles either.
The numbers 5 and 7 are **prime** numbers

b Write down **two** other numbers which are **prime** numbers.   .... , ...

       1 mark

c Melissa thinks that **15** is also a **prime** number.
Explain why she is **wrong**.

.... 1 mark

Level 6

4 A series of patterns is made out of **grey** and **red** counters.

Pattern number 1   Pattern number 2   Pattern number 3   Pattern number 4

a How many **grey** and **red** counters will there be in pattern number **6**?

.... grey counters .... red counters   1 mark

b How many **grey** and **red** counters will there be in pattern number **15**?

.... grey counters .... red counters   1 mark

c T = total number of grey and red counters in a pattern, N = pattern number.
Use symbols to write down an equation connecting T and N.

.... 1 mark

- **To find a formula for a sequence look at the differences between the terms.**

- **If those differences are the same, find the formula like this.**

  The rule is +3.

  The formula contains $3n$.
  $3n$ is the 3 times table.

  Write it underneath.

  You need to +1 to each multiple of 3
  to get the terms of the sequence.

  The formula for the nth term is $3n + 1$.

- **If these differences are not the same, look at the second differences.**

  If the second differences are the same the formula for the nth term will contain n^2.
  The number in front of the n^2 is half the second difference.

  The second differences are +4.
  The formula will start $2n^2$.

  Write down the sequence for $2n^2$.
  Write down what you need to add to
  each of these to get the terms of the
  sequence.
  Use the above method to find the
  formula for this new sequence.

  The formula is $3n - 1$

  Put the two parts together to get the
  formula for the sequence you started
  with.

  The formula is $2n^2 + 3n - 1$

Level 7

1 Find the formula for the nth term of this sequence

$$4 \qquad 11 \qquad 18 \qquad 25 \qquad 32$$

The formula contains ...... n

The formula is ....

2 The formula for the nth term of a sequence is $4n - 3$.
Write down

    a the first term $4 \times 1 - 3 = ...$

    b the sixth term $4 \times ... - 3 = ...$

    c the 20th term   .... $= ....$

3 Find the formula for the nth term of this sequence.

$$2 \qquad 8 \qquad 16 \qquad 26 \qquad 38$$

The formula will start ....

To get to the terms of
the sequence you need   ....

The formula is   ....

4 The formula for the nth term of a sequence is $3n^2 - n - 2$
Write down

    a the first term   ....

    b the fifth term   ....

1 This is a series of patterns made out of grey and blue tiles.

Pattern number 1   Pattern number 2   Pattern number 3

a How many grey and blue tiles will there be in pattern number 7?

.... grey tiles   .... blue tiles   1 mark

b How many grey and blue tiles will there be in pattern number 14?

.... grey tiles   .... blue tiles   1 mark

c Write expressions to show the total number of grey and blue tiles in pattern number n.

.... grey tiles   .... blue tiles   1 mark

d Write an expression to show the total number of tiles in pattern number n.

.... 1 mark

A different series of patterns is made with the grey and blue tiles.

Pattern number 1   Pattern number 2   Pattern number 3

e For this series of patterns write an expression to show the total number of tiles in pattern number n.
Show your working and simplify your expression.

Total number of tiles .... 2 marks

5　Formulas and equations

Letters can be used to represent numbers.

Levels 3–5

- **A formula is a set of instructions. It tells you how to work something out.**

- **A formula can be written using words or letters.**

  This formula tells you how to work out the cost, in pounds, of hiring a videotape.

  Cost = 3 × number of nights

  To hire a video for 2 nights

  Cost = 3 × 2 = £6

  This formula tells you how to work out the time, in minutes, needed to roast a turkey.

  Time = 25 + 15 × weight in pounds

  To roast a 12 lb turkey

  Time = 25 + 15 × 12 = 25 + 180 = 205 mins

- **This formula uses letters**
  The perimeter, p, of a square
  is given by $p = 4l$
  l is the length of a side of the square.
  Use the formula to find the perimeter
  of a square with sides of length 8 cm.

  $p = 4 × 8 = 32$ cm

- **You need to be able to write formulas yourself.**

  Pick out the important words and numbers.
  Choose letters to stand for the important words.

  The **cost** of a class trip to a theme park is £8 for each **pupil** and £100 for the coach.

  Use C for the cost and p for the number of pupils.

  The formula is $C = 100 + 8p$

Level 6

- **You can use trial and improvement to help you solve equations.**

  You guess different values and try to get closer to the answer.

  Solve $5x^2 - 20 = 1425$ using trial and improvement.

  Use a table to show your working.

Value of x	Value of $5x^2 - 20$	
10	$5 \times 10^2 - 20 = 480$	too small
20	$5 \times 20^2 - 20 = 1980$	too big
15	$5 \times 15^2 - 20 = 1105$	too small
17	$5 \times 17^2 - 20 = 1425$	correct

  Answer: $x = 17$

  The answer is the value of x in the left hand column, not the number 1425 you're trying to get closer to.

- **You can use trial and improvement to help you solve problems.**

  I think of a number, double it and add 23.
  The answer is 53. What number did I think of?

  Use a table to show your working.

Number	Answer	
10	$2 \times 10 + 23 = 43$	too small
20	$2 \times 20 + 23 = 63$	too big
15	$2 \times 15 + 23 = 53$	correct

  The number I thought of is 15.

- **You can use algebra to solve equations.** You need to get the letter by itself on one side of the equation. Look at what is being done to the letter. Do the opposite of this to both sides of the equation.

$x + 4 = 7$ take 4 from both sides $x + 4 - 4 = 7 - 4$ $x = 3$	$p - 3 = 12$ add 3 to both sides $p - 3 + 3 = 12 + 3$ $p = 15$
$5r = 35$ divide both sides by 5 $\dfrac{5r}{5} = \dfrac{35}{5}$ $r = 7$	$\dfrac{y}{6} = 4$ multiply both sides by 6 $\dfrac{y}{6} \times 6 = 4 \times 6$ $y = 24$

- **Some equations are more difficult.** More than one step is needed.

$2x + 7 = 16$ First, take 7 from both sides $2x + 7 - 7 = 16 - 7$ $2x = 9$ Now, divide both sides by 2 $\dfrac{2x}{2} = \dfrac{9}{2}$ $x = 4\frac{1}{2}$	$7x + 4 = 5x + 10$ This equation has xs on both sides First, take $5x$ from both sides $7x - 5x + 4 = 5x - 5x + 10$ $2x + 4 = 10$ Now take 4 from both sides $2x + 4 - 4 = 10 - 4$ $2x = 6$ divide both sides by 2 $x = 3$

- **When you have a bracket in an equation, get the bracket on its own first.**

Divide by 2 to get the bracket.

$$2(x + 7) = 18$$
$$x + 7 = 9$$
$$x = 2$$

Levels 3–5

1 a A plumber charges a call out charge of £25.
He then charges £15 an **hour**.
Write down the formula for the total **cost**.   ....

b Find the cost if the plumber is working for 4 hours.

....

2 Write down a formula for the perimeter, P,
of this rectangle.

w

l

....

Level 6

3 Solve $4x^2 - 27 = 1737$
by trial and improvement.

Value of x	Value of $4x^2 - 27$	
10	$4 \times 10^2 - 27 = ...$	too ...
20		

Answer $x = $ ......

4 Solve these equations

a $x + 7 = 13$

$x + 7$ ...... $= 13$ ......

$x = $ ......

c $5x - 28 = x - 6$

$5x$ ...... $- 28 = x$ ...... $- 6$

...... $- 28 = -6$

...... $= $ ....

$x = $ ......

b $\dfrac{x}{6} - 3 = 4$

$\dfrac{x}{6} - 3$ ...... $= 4$ ......

$\dfrac{x}{6} = $ ......

$\dfrac{x}{6} \times$ ...... $= $ ...... $\times$ ......

$x = $ ......

d $4(x - 3) = 28$

...... $= $ ......

$x = $ ......

1 Here are some expressions:

$$x \div 2 \quad x + 2 \quad x^3 \quad x + x \quad x^2 \quad 3x \quad x \times 2 \quad x \div 3 \quad x \div x \quad 2 + x$$

a Write down the expression that is the same as $x \times x$

.... 1 mark

b Write down the expression that is the same as $\dfrac{x}{3}$

.... 1 mark

c **Two** expressions are the same as $2x$.
Write down these two expressions

.... 1 mark

d Write down a **new** expression which will always be the same as $3x + x$.

.... 1 mark

2 There are n counters in a bag.

a Two of these bags, each with n counters, are put together to make a new bag.
Write an expression for the number of counters that are in the new bag.

.... 1 mark

b **Five** counters are then removed from the new bag.
Write an expression for the number of counters that are now in the new bag.

.... 1 mark

3 This **square** tile has edges of length n centimetres.
Six of the square tiles are put together to make a shape.

a Write an expression for the **perimeter** of the shape.
Simplify your expression.

.... cm   2 marks

b The perimeter of the shape is **60** cm.
Use your answer to part **a** to write an equation using **n**.
Solve your equation to find the **value of n**.

$n = $ ....   2 marks

4 Sapna had **3m** meal vouchers, but has used **4** of them.
Dale had **2m** meal vouchers, has used none, but has gained **one extra** voucher.

   a Write down **expressions**, in **m**, for the number of meal vouchers that
Sapna and Dale each have.

Sapna ....   Dale ....   2 marks

   b Sapna and Dale now have the **same** number of meal vouchers.
Write down an equation to show this.

....   1 mark

   c Solve the equation to find **m**.

$m = $ ....   1 mark

5 $y = x^2 + x - 3$

Find a value of x, to 1 dp, that gives the value of y closest to 0.
Two values for x have already been worked out.

x	1	2					
y	-1	3					

$x = $ ....

- **The signs < ≤ > ≥ are all called inequality signs.**
  < means less than   > means greater than
  ≤ means less than or equal to   ≥ means greater than or equal to

- **You can show inequalities on a number line.**

$$x \leqslant 3$$

$$20 \leqslant x < 50$$

- **You solve inequalities like equations.**

$$4x - 6 \geqslant 11$$

$$4x - 6 + 6 \geqslant 11 + 6$$

$$4x \geqslant 17$$

$$x \geqslant \frac{17}{4}$$

$$\frac{x}{3} + 4 < 2$$

$$\frac{x}{3} + 4 - 4 < 2 - 4$$

$$\frac{x}{3} < -2$$

$$x < -6$$

- **Sometimes you have to give possible values.**
  If $-4 \leqslant x < 3$ and x is an integer
  then x can take the values $-4, -3, -2, -1, 0, 1, 2$.
  An integer is a whole number.

- **Inequalities can have two variables, usually x and y.**

  These can be shown using a graph
  The red line is $y = 2x + 1$
  The red shading shows $y \geqslant 2x + 1$

  The blue line is $y = x - 2$
  The blue shading shows $y < x - 2$
  The line is dashed to show that
  it is not included.

- **A region can be described using more than one inequality.**

  Show the region given by

  $-2 < x \leq 3 \qquad y < 1 \qquad y \geq x - 2$

  You can shade the parts that you don't want.
  The answer is the region, R, which is not shaded.

  Always make it clear on your diagram
  which is the required region.

- **Substituting into formulas.**

  You need to be able to deal with fractions, decimals and negative numbers.

  Remember that you can use the $a\frac{b}{c}$ key on your calculator to deal with fractions.

  If $y = 4x^2 - 3$ find y when

  a $x = \frac{3}{4}$ **b** $x = 2.7$ **c** $x = -5$

a $y = 4 \times (\frac{3}{4})^2 - 3$	**b** $y = 4 \times (2.7)^2 - 3$	**c** $y = 4 \times (-5)^2 - 3$
$\quad = 4 \times \frac{9}{16} - 3$	$\quad = 4 \times 7.29 - 3$	$\quad = 4 \times 25 - 3$
$\quad = -\frac{3}{4}$	$\quad = 26.16$	$\quad = 97$

- **Changing the subject of a formula.**
  This works like solving equations.
  Get the new subject letter by itself.
  Write the new formula with the subject letter on the left hand side.

  Make s the subject.   Make b the subject.

  $p = 3s - r \qquad\qquad\qquad a = \sqrt{b + 3c}$

  $p + r = 3s \qquad\qquad\qquad a^2 = b + 3c$

  $\dfrac{p + r}{3} = s \qquad\qquad\qquad a^2 - 3c = b$

  $s = \dfrac{p + r}{3} \qquad\qquad\qquad b = a^2 - 3c$

- **Factorising by taking out common factors.**
  This is the reverse of multiplying out brackets.

  Factorise

  a $18 - 12p$　　**b** $12a^3 - 4a^2$

  a $18 - 12p = 6(3 - 2p)$
  6 is the highest common factor,
  HCF, of 18 and 12

  b $12a^3 - 4a^2 = 4a^2(3a - 1)$
  a^2 is the HCF of a^3 and a^2
  Notice the 1 at the end of the bracket

- **Multiplying out 2 brackets.** You multiply the second bracket by each term in the first bracket.

$$(s + 3)(2s - 5) = s(2s - 5) + 3(2s - 5) \qquad (x + 4)^2 = (x + 4)(x + 4)$$
$$= 2s^2 - 5s + 6s - 15 \qquad\qquad\quad = x^2 + 4x + 4x + 16$$
$$= 2s^2 + s - 15 \qquad\qquad\qquad\quad = x^2 + 8x + 16$$

- **You can use trial and improvement to solve more complicated equations.**
  Sometimes answers do not work out exactly.

  Example　Solve $x^2 = 135$　giving your answer to 1 dp.

Value of x	Value of x^2	
11	121	too small
12	144	too big
11.5	132.25	too small
11.6	134.56	too small
11.7	136.89	too big
11.65	135.7225	too big

x is between 11 and 12
x is between 11.5 and 12
x is between 11.6 and 12
x is between 11.6 and 11.7
x is between 11.6 and 11.65

```
 |  |  |  |  |  |  |  |  |  |
11.6         11.65        11.7
```

x must be somewhere in the green part of the number line. Any number in the green part rounds down to 11.6 to 1 dp.

Answer:　$x = 11.6$ to 1 dp.

Level 7

1 Solve these inequalities and show your answers on number lines.

a $2x + 3 \leqslant 11$

$2x \leqslant \dots$

$\dots$

b $\dfrac{x}{5} - 2 > 1$

$\dots > \dots$

$\dots$

2 If $-1 < x \leqslant 4$ and x is an integer then x can take the values $\dots$

Level 8

3 Write down the inequalities shown by the shading.

a

b

c

4 Make r the subject of

a $x = 2r - c^2$

$\dots = 2r$

$\dots$

$r = \dots$

b $p = (r - s)^2$

$\dots = (r - s)$

$\dots$

$\dots$

5 Factorise

a $14q - 8$

$\dots$

b $16a^3 - 8a$

$\dots$

6 Multiply out

a $(x + 4)(x - 3)$

$\dots$

$\dots$

b $(2x - 3)(x - 6)$

$\dots$

$\dots$

1 The table shows the result of adding pairs of expressions.
Complete the table.

A	B	A + B
x	y	
$3a$	$5a$	
$2p$		$2p - 5q$
$5x + 2y$	$3y - 4w$	
	$6k$	$2k$
x^2	$3x^2$	

3 marks

2 A weatherman reported, 'The temperature this
summer never quite reached 24 degrees.'
a Shade the temperature scale to show
the **maximum** temperature.

1 mark

b T = temperature
Write down an inequality, using T,
to show the statement of the weatherman.

....

1 mark

c The temperature for the winter months
could be represented by the diagram

Write down an inequality, using T,
to show this range of temperature.

....

1 mark

3 Find the values of P and Q when $x = 5$ and $y = 3$

a $P = \dfrac{x^2(x - 1)}{4}$ **b** $Q = \dfrac{5y^3}{6}$

$P = \ldots\ldots$ $Q = \ldots\ldots$

2 marks

4 The diagram shows a **square**.
The expressions show the length of a
side of the square, in centimetres.

Calculate the value of x, and use it to
find the area of the square.

.... cm^2 2 marks

Level 8

5 The diagram shows
some straight line graphs.

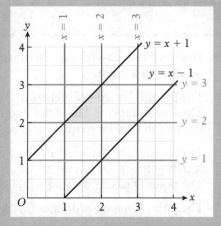

  a Write down **three** inequalities
  which can be used to describe
  the shaded region.   3 marks

  b On the diagram shade the region
  which is described by the inequalities

  $y \geqslant 1$ $y \leqslant x - 1$ $x \leqslant 3$ 2 marks

6 Multiply out and simplify these expressions:

  a $2(x - 3) - (x - 7)$ **b** $(x - 2)(x + 3)$ **c** $(x + 5)^2$ 3 marks

7 Solve these equations.

  a $5 - 3x = 6x + 11$ **b** $2(x - 1) = 6$ **c** $\dfrac{3x}{x - 1} = 5$

  $x = $ .... $x = $ .... $x = $ ....   6 marks

6 Functions and graphs

You use co-ordinates to find the position of a point.

Levels 3–5

- **You need two co-ordinates to describe the position of a point.**

  The point P has co-ordinates (3, 2).
  The first number is called the x co-ordinate.
  It tells you how far to move across.

  The second number is called the y co-ordinate.
  It tells you how far to move up.
  The point Q has co-ordinates (2, 0).

  The point R has co-ordinates (0, 3).

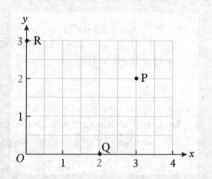

Level 6

- **Negative numbers are also used in co-ordinates.**
  If the x co-ordinate is negative it tells you to move to the left.
  If the y co-ordinate is negative it tells you to move down.

  The co-ordinates are
  Sun   (0, 0)
  Mercury (−1, 1)
  Venus   (2, −1)
  Earth   (−2, −2)

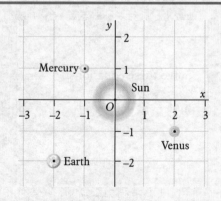

- **To draw a graph**
  (1) Make a table of values.
  (2) Plot the points and join them up.

  Draw the graph of $y = 2x + 1$

x	−1	0	1	2
y	−1	1	3	5

  ↑   ↑
  $2 \times (-1) + 1$ $2 \times 1 + 1$

- **The equation of any straight line can be written as $y = mx + c$**

  m is the gradient of the line. It tells you how steep the line is. c is where the line crosses the y axis.

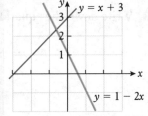

  The red line has gradient 1
  and crosses the y axis at 3.

  The blue line has gradient -2
  and crosses the y axis at 1.

- **Vertical lines have equations starting $x =$**

- **Horizontal lines have equations starting $y =$**

- **Parallel lines have the same gradient.**

- **Checking to see if a point lies on a line.**
  Does the point $(2, 5)$ lie on the line $y = 3x - 2$?
  When $x = 2$, $y = 3 \times 2 - 2 = 4$
  so $(2, 4)$ lies on the line.
  $(2, 5)$ does not lie on the line.

- **Some equations do not have y on its own.**
  To draw the graph of $3x + 4y = 12$
  find where the graph crosses each axis

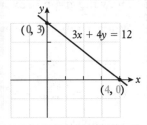

  When $x = 0$ When $y = 0$
  $4y = 12$ $3x = 12$
  $y = 3$ $x = 4$
  This gives $(0, 3)$ This gives $(4, 0)$

1 Fill in the co-ordinates

A (......, ...)   B (......, ...)   C (......, ...)

2 Plot these points
D (1, 3)   E (4, 5)   F (3, 0)

3 Write down the equation of the red line

....

4 Write down the equation of each of these lines.
Choose from
$y = -x$, $y = 2x + 2$, $x = 2$, $y = -x - 3$

A ....   C ....

B ....   D ....

5 Draw the graph of $3x - 2y = 6$

When $x = 0$ When $y = 0$

.... = ... = ...

.... = ... = ...

This gives (......, ...)   This gives (......, ...)

PRACTICE QUESTIONS

1 These triangles make a pattern on a grid.
Each triangle is numbered.
The **bottom right hand corner** of each
triangle is marked with a letter.

   a Write down the coordinates of the
       corner marked

        A (,   )   B (,   )   C (,   )   2 marks

   b What are the co-ordinates of the bottom right hand corner of triangle **number 10**?

       (,   )

       Explain how you worked out your answer.

                                  2 marks

   c Explain why **(10, 9) cannot** be a **corner** of a triangle.

                                    1 mark

2 a Plot each of the points P, Q, R and S
     on the grid. Join the points together
     with straight lines.

     P (0, 0)   R (2, 2)
     Q (0, 2)   S (2, 0)

                                    2 marks

   b Give the name of the **shape** that you have drawn.

                           .... 1 mark

c Multiply each of the co-ordinates P, Q, R and S **by 3**, and plot these points on the same axes

P (0, 0) × 3 → (,)

Q (0, 2) × 3 → (,)

R (2, 2) × 3 → (,)

S (2, 0) × 3 → (,)   2 marks

d How many **times larger** is the **area** of this shape, compared with the area of the original shape?

.... 1 mark

Level 6

3 The diagram shows the graph of the straight line $y = x + 1$.

a Draw the graph of the straight line $y = x + 2$.
Label your graph.   1 mark

b Draw the graph of the straight line $y = 2x + 2$.
Label your graph.   1 mark

c Write down the equation of any straight line which goes through (0, 0).

$y = $ .... 1 mark

d Write down the equation of a straight line which is parallel to $y = x + 1$, and goes through $(-2, 5)$.

$y = $ .... 1 mark

- **The point where two lines cross is called the point of intersection.**
  These lines cross at the point $(2, 3)$

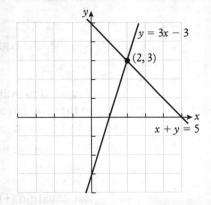

- $x = 2$, $y = 3$ is the solution to the simultaneous equations

$$y = 3x - 3$$
$$x + y = 5$$

- **To solve a pair of simultaneous equations**

  either   draw the graphs of the 2 equations and find where they cross
  or   use algebra.

- **Solving simultaneous equations using algebra.**

Solve   (1) $5x + y = 20$
        (2) $2x + y = 11$

Solve   (1) $3x + y = 19$
        (2) $x - y = 1$

Subtract the equations to get rid of y

$$3x = 9$$
$$x = 3$$

Add the equations to get rid of y

$$4x = 20$$
$$x = 5$$

Put $x = 3$ into (1) to find y

$$5 \times 3 + y = 20$$
$$y = 5$$

Put $x = 5$ into (1) to find y

$$3 \times 5 + y = 19$$
$$y = 4$$

The solution is $x = 3, y = 5$

The solution is $x = 5, y = 4$

Use (2) to check your answer

$$2x + y = 2 \times 3 + 5$$
$$= 11 \checkmark$$

Use (2) to check your answer

$$x - y = 5 - 4$$
$$= 1 \checkmark$$

- **You sometimes need to multiply one or both of the equations before you add or subtract.**

Solve this pair of simultaneous equations

$$2x + 3y = 13$$
$$4x - y = 5$$

Number the equations

(1) $2x + 3y = 13$
(2) $4x - y = 5$

You need to multiply equation (2) by **3**
so that you have $3y$ in
each equation

$$2x + 3y = 13$$
$(2) \times 3$ $12x - 3y = 15$

Add to get rid of y

$$14x = 28$$

This finds x

$$x = 2$$

Use equation (1) to find y

Put $x = 2$ in equation (1)

$$2 \times 2 + 3y = 13$$
$$4 + 3y = 13$$
$$3y = 9$$
$$y = 3$$

The answer is $x = 2$, $y = 3$

Use equation (2) to
check your answer

Check $4x - y = 4 \times 2 - 3$
$$= 5 \checkmark$$

Solve this pair of simultaneous equations

$$3x + 5y = 30$$
$$2x + 3y = 19$$

Number the equations

(1) $3x + 5y = 30$
(2) $2x + 3y = 19$

Multiply equation (1) by 2
Multiply equation (2) by 3

$$6x + 10y = 60$$
$$6x + 9y = 57$$

You can now subtract to get rid of x
Put $y = 3$ in equation (1)

$$y = 3$$
$$3x + 15 = 30$$
$$3x = 15$$
$$x = 5$$

The answer is $x = 5$, $y = 3$

Check using equation (2)

Check $2x + 3y = 2 \times 5 + 3 \times 3$
$$= 19 \checkmark$$

● **You need to be able to recognise these graphs.**

Any quadratic graph will look like ∨ or ∧
An equation for a quadratic graph will have an x^2 term but no higher powers of x.

Other cubic graphs will look like one of these or ⋎ or ⋏
An equation for a cubic graph will have an x^3 term but no higher powers of x.

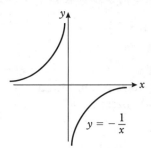

All reciprocal graphs will look like one of these.
Reciprocal graphs always have two parts.

● **Look for these features when describing or sketching graphs that model real situations,** e.g. filling containers with liquid, speed around a track.

steady increase

steady decrease

increasing but rate of increase slowing down

decreasing but rate of decrease slowing down

increasing and rate of increase speeding up

decreasing and rate of decrease speeding up

no change

● **You can describe a graph using these features.**

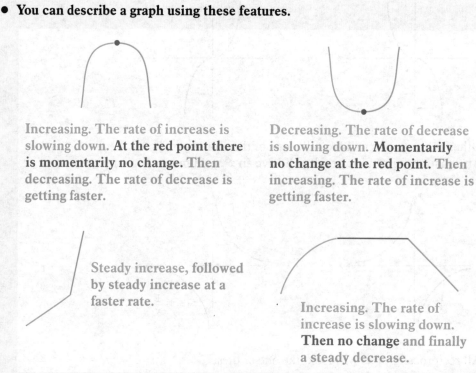

Increasing. The rate of increase is slowing down. **At the red point there is momentarily no change. Then** decreasing. The rate of decrease is getting faster.

Decreasing. The rate of decrease is slowing down. **Momentarily no change at the red point. Then** increasing. The rate of increase is getting faster.

Steady increase, followed by steady increase at a faster rate.

Increasing. The rate of increase is slowing down. **Then no change** and finally a steady decrease.

1 Solve these pairs of simultaneous equations:

a (1) $2x + y = 14$
(2) $3x - y = 6$

Adding   ...... = ...

$x = ...$

Put $x = ...$ into (1)

$2 \times ...... + y = ...$

$y = ...$

the solution is $x = ...$, $y = ...$

Check in (2)

$3 \times ...... - ...... = ...$

b (1) $4x + 2y = 10$
(2) $5x + 3y = 12$

Multiply (1) by ...... and (2) by ......

...... = ...

...... = ...

Subtracting   ...... = ...

...... = ...

Put ...... = ... into (1)

...... = ...

...... = ...

the solution is ....

Check in (2) ....

2 Write down the letter of the graph by its equation.

A

B

C

D

$y = x^3 - 6x^2 + 11x - 6$

Graph ......

$y = 4 - x^2$

Graph ......

$y = x^2 - 4x + 7$

Graph ......

$y = \dfrac{1}{x - 3}$

Graph ......

3 This flask is filled with water at a constant rate.
Sketch the graph to show how the height of the water changes and explain the features of your graph.

Height of water | Time

....

....

....

....

PRACTICE QUESTIONS

1 a Write down the **equation** of the line

through A and B ....

Write down the **equation** of the line

through B and C ....

2 marks

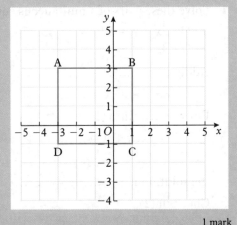

b Fill in the gaps below:

$y - x = 2$ is the equation of the line

through .... and ....   1 mark

c One of the lines of symmetry of the square is $x = -1$.
On the diagram, **draw and label** the line $x = -1$.   1 mark

Write down the equation of **one other** line of symmetry.

.... 1 mark

d The line $y - x = 2$ crosses the line $2y + x = 22$

Solve the simultaneous equations (1) $2y + x = 22$
Show your working.   (2) $y - x = 2$

$x = ...$ $y = ...$ 2 marks

e Write down the co-ordinates of the point where the line $y - x = 2$ crosses the
line $2y + x = 22$.

(......, ...) 1 mark

2 Solve these simultaneous equations to find the value of x and y.

(1) $8x + 6y\ \ \ \ \ = 10$
(2) $30x - 6y + 1 = 10$

Show your working.

$x = ...$ $y = ...$ 3 marks

3 The diagram shows the graphs of the equations

$$4y = x + 2$$
$$4y = -x + 6$$

Use the diagram to write down the solutions to these simultaneous equations.

$x = $ ...... $y = $ ......   2 marks

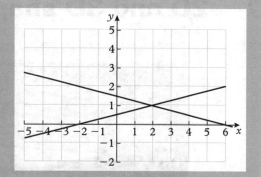

Level 8

4 The diagram shows the graph with the equation $y = 2x^2$.

a On the same axes draw the graph with the equation $y = x^2$.

b On the same axes draw the graph with the equation $y = 2x^2 + 2$

c On the same axes draw the graph with the equation $y = -2x^2$.

3 marks

5 The graph shows the journey of a car between two sets of traffic lights.

Describe in detail what happened during the journey of the car, as shown by the graph.

....

....

....

3 marks

7   2D and 3D shapes

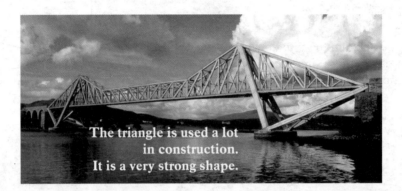

The triangle is used a lot in construction.
It is a very strong shape.

Levels 3–5

- **Types of angle**

Right angle
90°

Straight line
180°

Full turn
360°

Acute angle
less than 90°

Obtuse angle
between 90° and 180°

Reflex angle
greater than 180°

- **Points of the compass**

- **Directions of turn**

clockwise   anti-clockwise

- **You need to be able to use a protractor or angle measurer**

- **Angles on a straight line add up to 180°.**

  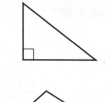

  the red angle must be 80° because 100 + 80 = 180

- **The angles in a triangle add up to 180°.**

  the blue angle must be 50° because 90 + 40 + 50 = 180

- **Types of triangle**

  Right angled triangle

  Equilateral triangle
  All 3 sides are equal
  All 3 angles are equal

  Scalene triangle
  No equal sides
  No equal angles

  Isosceles triangle
  2 sides are equal
  2 angles are equal

- **Constructing triangles**

  Always leave your construction lines on your diagram.

  Given 3 sides:
  Draw the longest side
  Use compasses to draw the 2 red arcs
  Join up the triangle

  1.5 cm   2 cm
  3 cm

  Given 1 side and 2 angles:
  Draw the side
  Use a protractor to draw the 2 angles
  This will complete the triangle.

  40°   50°
  3 cm

  Given 2 sides and 1 angle:
  Draw the longest side
  Use a protractor to draw the angle
  Mark the length of the other side
  Join up the triangle.

  2.5 cm
  45°
  3 cm

- **Two shapes are congruent if they are exactly the same.**

- **Types of quadrilateral**
  A shape with 4 straight sides is a quadrilateral.

square
All 4 sides equal
All 4 angles are 90°

rectangle
2 pairs of equal sides
All 4 angles are 90°

parallelogram
Opposite sides equal and parallel
Opposite angles are equal

kite
2 pairs of equal sides
1 pair of equal angles

trapezium
1 pair of parallel sides

rhombus
All 4 sides equal
Opposite angles equal

- **Drawings of 3D shapes**

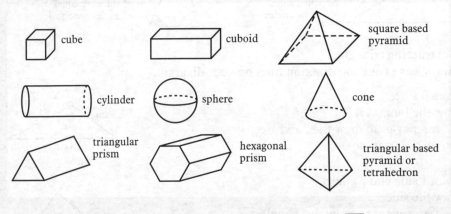

cube

cuboid

square based pyramid

cylinder

sphere

cone

triangular prism

hexagonal prism

triangular based pyramid or tetrahedron

- **A prism is a solid that has the same cross section all the way through.**

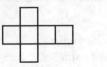

- **When a solid is opened out and laid flat, the shape that you get is called a net of the solid.**

This net   would make   this cube.

- **Names of polygons**

  3 sides – triangle   5 sides – pentagon   8 sides – octagon
  4 sides – quadrilateral   6 sides – hexagon   10 sides – decagon

- A polygon is regular if all its sides are the same length and all its angles are equal.

- The angles of a quadrilateral add up to 360°.

The red angle is 80° because

$$110 + 50 + 120 + 80 = 360$$

- The exterior angles of a polygon add up to 360°. If the hexagon is regular,

each red angle $= \dfrac{360}{6} = 60°$

The red angles add up to 360°

- The angles inside a polygon are called interior angles.
They always make a straight line with the exterior angle.

Exterior angle + Interior angle = 180°

If the pentagon is regular, each red angle $= \dfrac{360}{5} = 72°$

so each blue angle $= 180 - 72 = 108°$

- **Angles between intersecting lines**
The red angles are equal.
The blue angles are equal.
Each pair of angles is called vertically opposite angles or X angles.

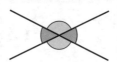

- **Angles between parallel lines**

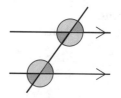

The red angles are equal.
The blue angles are equal.
These angles are called **alternate angles** or Z angles.

The red angles are equal.
The blue angles are equal.
These angles are called **corresponding angles** or F angles.

All the red acute angles are equal.

All the blue obtuse angles are equal.

A red and a blue angle together add up to 180°.

TEST YOURSELF

Levels 3–5

1 Write down the name of each of these angles.

a

b

c

....

2 An aeroplane is flying due south. What direction will it be flying if it turns

a 90° clockwise .... **c** 270° clockwise ....

b 45° anticlockwise .... **d** 135° anticlockwise ....

3 Find the red angle.

a ....

b ....

c ....

Level 6

4 Sketch each of these
  a Cuboid   **b** Cylinder   **c** Square-based pyramid

5 Find
  a the red angle   **b** the blue angle

....

6 Find each of the coloured angles

  a red angle = ...

  b blue angle = ...

  c green angle = ...

72

Levels 3–5

1 A cardboard box is being made for a small toy.
A plan of the **net** of the box is drawn first.

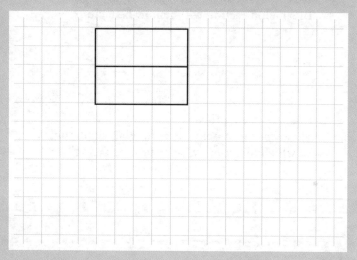

a **Complete** the plan of the **net**.   3 marks

b A **flap** is to be added so the box can have a **top** which closes.
Add the **flap** to your plan of the **net**.   1 mark

2

a Which is the **smallest** angle?   .... 1 mark

b Which is the **largest** angle?   .... 1 mark

c Which **two** angles are the **same size**?   .... and .... 1 mark

d Which angle is a **right angle**?   .... 1 mark

e Draw an angle which is an **obtuse** angle.

1 mark

3 a John is facing **South**.
He turns **clockwise** through **2 right angles**.
In which direction will he now be facing?

.... 1 mark

b Louise is facing **East**.
She turns **anticlockwise** through **3 right angles**.
In which direction will she now be facing?

.... 1 mark

Level 6

4 a

Calculate angles *a*, *b* and *c*.

a = ... *b* = ... *c* = ...   3 marks

b

Calculate angles *d*, *e* and *f*.

d = ... *e* = ... *f* = ...   3 marks

What is the name of the blue shape?

.... 1 mark

- **Pythagoras' theorem** is used to find the length of a side in a right angled triangle. You use it when you know the length of two of the sides.

- The **hypotenuse**, h, is the longest side of a right angled triangle.

- Pythagoras' theorem tells you

    $$h^2 = a^2 + b^2$$

    The square of the hypotenuse = the sum of the squares of the other two sides

- **Finding the hypotenuse**

    $$h^2 = 8^2 + 11^2$$
    $$= 64 + 121$$
    $$= 185$$
    $$h = \sqrt{185}$$
    $$= 13.6 \text{ cm} \ (3 \text{ sf})$$

    Check that your answer for the hypotenuse is longer than each of the other two sides.

- **Finding one of the shorter sides.**
    Always start by writing Pythagoras theorem in the usual order starting with hypotenuse$^2 = \ldots$

    $$25^2 = x^2 + 9^2$$
    $$25^2 - 9^2 = x^2$$
    $$x^2 = 625 - 81$$
    $$= 544$$
    $$x = \sqrt{544}$$
    $$= 23.3 \text{ cm} \ (3 \text{ sf})$$

    Check that your answer is shorter than the hypotenuse.

75

- **Trigonometry is used to find the length of a side or an angle in a right angled triangle.**

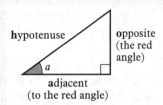

- **The 3 trig ratios are**

$$\sin a = \frac{\text{opp}}{\text{hyp}} \quad \cos a = \frac{\text{adj}}{\text{hyp}} \quad \tan a = \frac{\text{opp}}{\text{adj}}$$

- **Finding a length**

$$\sin 40° = \frac{x}{5}$$

$$5 \times \sin 40° = x$$

$$x = 3.21 \text{ m} \quad (3 \text{ sf})$$

- **Finding an angle**

$$\tan a = \frac{12}{18}$$

$$a = 33.7° \quad (1 \text{ dp})$$

- **Bearings are always measured clockwise starting from North. A bearing must always have 3 figures.**

Bearing of B from A = 120°

Bearing of B from A = 050°

Bearing of B from A = 210°

Bearing of B from A = 300°

- **Bearings are often used in trigonometry questions.**
  Use the bearing to find the angle to work with.

A ship travels 100 miles on a bearing of 204°. How far South does it travel?

$$\cos 24° = \frac{x}{100} \qquad x = 91.4 \text{ miles (3 sf)}$$

Level 7

1 Find x in each of these.

a

8 cm

x

13 cm

$x^2 = \ldots\ldots + \ldots\ldots$

$ = \ldots\ldots$

$x = \sqrt{\ldots\ldots}$

$x = \ldots\ldots$ (3 sf)

b

x

7.8 cm

12.3 cm

$\ldots\ldots = \ldots\ldots + \ldots\ldots$

$\ldots\ldots - \ldots\ldots = \ldots\ldots$

$x^2 = \ldots\ldots$

$x = \sqrt{\ldots\ldots}$

$x = \ldots\ldots$ (3 sf)

Level 8

2 Find p in each of these.

a

14.1 m

38°

p

$\ldots\ldots\, 38° = \dfrac{p}{\ldots\ldots}$

$\ldots\ldots\ldots = p$

$p = \ldots\ldots$ m (3 sf)

b

17 cm

p

11 cm

$\ldots\ldots\, p = \dfrac{\ldots\ldots}{\ldots\ldots}$

$p = \ldots\ldots$ cm (1 dp)

3 A plane flies 500 miles on a bearing of 306° from A. How far west does it travel?

N

A

....

....

....

1 This shape is a **square-based** pyramid.

Write down the letter of the **one** net which can be used to make this pyramid.

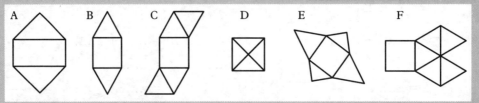

1 mark

2 A boat is to sail around a hexagonal course ABCDEF, past 6 buoys. The boat starts from point A.

   a Through what angle x should the boat turn at each of the buoys?

$x = $ .... 1 mark

   b What bearing y should the boat sail on at the start of the race?

$y = $ .... 1 mark

3 **Calculate** the area of the triangle.

Area = ... cm^2 3 marks

5 A boat is sailed around a lake.

Point C is 350 metres due North of A.
Point B is 450 metres due West of A.

a Calculate the direct distance from point B to point C.

.... m   2 marks

b Calculate the bearing the boat must sail on to travel from point B to point C.

.... °   2 marks

c Calculate the bearing the boat must sail on to travel from point C to point B.

.... °   1 mark

d The boat sails on a bearing of 60° from point B, across the lake until it reaches point D, due North of A.
Calculate the distance from B to D.

.... m   2 marks

8 Position and movement

The window acts like a mirror. The reflection makes it look as though this woman has both feet off the ground.

Levels 3–5

- A line of symmetry divides a shape into two identical halves.
  Each half is a reflection of the other.
  If you fold a shape along a line of symmetry each half fits exactly on top of the other.

- A shape can have more than 1 line of symmetry or none at all.

A rectangle has
2 lines of symmetry

A square has
4 lines of symmetry

A parallelogram does not
have any lines of symmetry

The dashed red lines are the lines of symmetry.
They are sometimes called mirror lines.

- **To reflect a shape in a mirror line**
  (1) Reflect each corner in turn.
      The new position must be the
      same distance on the other
      side of the mirror line.
      Use the squares to help you.
  (2) Join these points to get the
      reflected shape.

- **You can reflect 3-D shapes in a mirror.**
  This shape is symmetrical about the mirror.

- A shape has **rotational symmetry** if it fits on top of itself more than once as it makes a complete turn.

- The **order of rotational symmetry** is the number of times the shape fits on top of itself.

- The **centre of rotation** is the point at the centre of the shape that stays still as the shape turns.

A rectangle has rotational symmetry of order 2 | A square has rotational symmetry of order 4 | A parallelogram has no rotational symmetry

- **To rotate a shape about any point.**
  (1) You need to know the angle and the direction of turn.
  (2) Trace the shape.
  (3) Put your pencil on the centre of rotation and rotate the tracing paper.
  (4) Draw the shape in its new position.

Tracing paper

Traced triangle being rotated

Normal paper

Pencil holding centre of rotation in place

Original triangle

You can use a cross on the tracing paper to help you see when you have rotated through 90°, 180°, 270°.

- A **translation** is a movement in a straight line. The shape A has been moved 3 squares to the right and 1 square down to get to B.

- **When you are doing more than 1 transformation on a shape make sure you do them in the right order.**

- **An enlargement changes the size of a shape.**
  The change is the same in all directions.

- **The scale factor tells you how many times bigger the enlargement is.**
  Rectangle B is an enlargement of rectangle A, scale factor 2.

- This map shows some streets.
  The real streets are an enlargement of the map.
  The scale of the map tells you the scale factor of the enlargement.
  The distance between the church and the school on the map is 2 cm.
  To find the actual distance multiply by the scale factor

  Actual distance = 2 × 10 000 cm
  $\qquad\qquad\qquad$ = 20 000 cm
  $\qquad\qquad\qquad$ = 200 m

Level 6

- **An enlargement can be done from a point.**
  This point is called the centre of enlargement, C.
  Look at the corner of the small triangle marked ●
  ● is 1 square from C.
  The new position will be 1 × 3 = 3 squares from C.
  Do the same for the other corners of the shape.

- **Symmetry of the regular polygons.**

Equilateral triangle	Square	Regular pentagon
3 lines of symmetry rotational symmetry of order 3	4 lines of symmetry rotational symmetry of order 4	5 lines of symmetry rotational symmetry of order 5

Regular hexagon	Regular octagon	Regular decagon
6 lines of symmetry rotational symmetry of order 6	8 lines of symmetry rotational symmetry of order 8	10 lines of symmetry rotational symmetry of order 10

- **Symmetry of solids**
  This is a cuboid.
  You can see the three possible
  places to put a mirror so that
  the two halves are
  symmetrical.
  When you put a mirror into a
  shape like this the mirror is
  called a plane of symmetry.

1 For each of these shapes draw the lines of symmetry and write down the order of rotational symmetry.

a

b

c

d

order ......   order ......   order ......   order ......

2 a Translate triangle A 6 squares to the right and 2 squares up.

   b Rotate triangle A 90° clockwise about ●

   c Reflect triangle A in the blue line.

3 Enlarge this shape using centre C and scale factor 2.

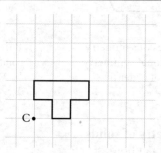

4 Write down the number of planes of symmetry.

a

b

c

square-based pyramid

....

Levels 3–5

1 a Shade in **1 more square** to make a shape which has line AB as a **line of symmetry**.

1 mark

b Shade in **1 more square** to make a shape with line CD as a **line of symmetry**.

1 mark

c Shade in **3 more squares** to make a shape which has **two lines of symmetry**.

1 mark

d Shade in **1 more square** to make a shape which has **rotational symmetry**.

1 mark

e Shade in 3 more squares to make a shape which has **two lines of symmetry** and **rotational symmetry** about the marked point.

1 mark

f Shade A has been **rotated clockwise** onto shape B. Mark with a clear cross the **centre of rotation**.

Write down the angle of rotation.

....

2 marks

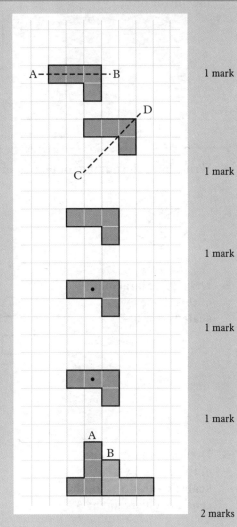

2 For each of these patterns draw in **all the lines of symmetry**.

a   **b**   **c**

3 marks

3 Reflect this triangle in the mirror line.

2 marks

Level 6

4 Write down the number of **planes of symmetry** in the following solids.

a

Cube ....

b

Prism ....

2 marks

5 Draw an **enlargement** of this shape by a **scale factor** of 2.

3 marks

6 Draw an **enlargement** of this shape by a **scale factor** of **3** from the centre of enlargement A.

•A

2 marks

- **An enlargement can also make a shape smaller.**
  This happens when the scale factor is between 0 and 1. Shape A has been enlarged by scale factor $\frac{1}{2}$.

- **The locus of an object is all the possible positions that the object can take as it moves according to a rule.**
  You can describe a locus in words or with a diagram.
  The red line shows the locus in each of these.

Points that are 1.5 cm from A.

A circle, centre A radius 1.5 cm.

Points that are equidistant from the two points A and B.

The perpendicular bisector of the line AB.

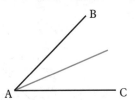

Points that are equidistant from the lines AB and AC.

The bisector of angle BAC.

Points that are 1 cm from the line AB.

Pair of parallel lines with a semicircle at each end.

- **You can also shade regions to show where something can be.**
  The red region shows the points that are nearer to A than to B.

- **Two triangles are similar if they have the same angles.**
  Triangles P and Q are similar.

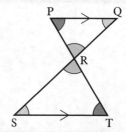

The red angles are corresponding angles so they are equal.
The blue angles are corresponding angles so they are equal.
Triangles ABC and ADE are similar.

The red and blue angles are alternate angles so they are equal.
The green angles are opposite angles and so they are equal.
Triangles PQR and TSR are similar.

- **Similar triangles are enlargements of each other.**
  Use the scale factor to find missing lengths.
  Make sure you're working with corresponding sides.

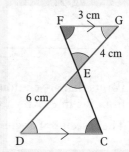

Triangles CDE and FGE are similar.
GE and ED are corresponding sides as they are both opposite the red angles.
The scale factor for the enlargement from FGE to CDE is 6 ÷ 4 = 1.5.
GF and CD are corresponding sides
Length CD = 3 × 1.5
= 4.5 cm.

Level 7

1 Enlarge the shape
using centre C and
scale factor $\frac{1}{2}$.

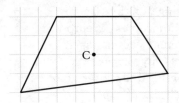

2 The diagram shows a wheel.
  a Draw the locus of the red point on the rim of the wheel as the wheel rolls along
the line.
  b Draw the locus of the blue point at the centre of the wheel.

3 An ambulance station must be less
than 4 km from the hospital and
less than 3 km from the motorway.
Show the region where it could be.

Hospital

Scale: 1 cm to 2 km   Motorway

Level 8

4 **a** Mark the pairs of equal angles.
  b Write down the corresponding side to

    (1) PQ ......   (2) SR ....

  c Find the scale factor for the
enlargement from RST to PQR.

    ...... ÷ ...... = ...

  d Find the length SR.

    ...... ÷ ...... = ... cm

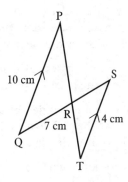

1 This is a logo measuring 7 cm by 10 cm.
June wants to use a photocopier to reproduce
the logo on three different sizes of paper.
The logo needs to be as large as possible
on each sheet of paper. Find the scale factor
she should use for each size of paper.
Give your answers correct to 2 dp.

a ←—42 cm—→
30 cm

....

b ←—30 cm—→
21 cm

....

c ←—21cm—→
15 cm

....

3 marks

2

A ←— 6 m —→ B
3 m
D   C

This is a plan of a garden plot.
Draw an **accurate scale plan** of the plot.
Use a scale of 1 square to represent 1 m.

1 mark

a A row of flowers is planted in a **straight line** exactly **1.5 m** from the side BC.
Show the location of the line of flowers on your scale plan.

1 mark

b The plot is divided by a small fence. The fence starts in corner D, and runs
across the plot so as to be the same distance from side AD and side DC.
On your scale plan show the position of the fence.

1 mark

c Seeds are sown in such a way as to be no more than 1 metre from corner A.
On your scale plan shade the location in which the seeds can be sown.

1 mark

3 This is an accurate plan of a garden pond.
It has been drawn using a scale of 1 cm to represent 1 m.

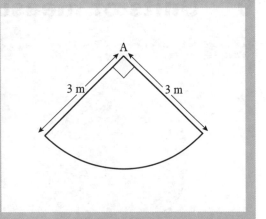

a A fence is to be put up which is **exactly 1 metre** from the edge of the pond. Draw **accurately** the position of the fence on the scale plan. 3 marks

b A small fountain is at the corner A of the pond. It sprays water up to one metre away. On the scale plan shade the part of the pond which is sprayed by the fountain.

1 mark

Level 8

4 These two tins are mathematically similar. The external dimensions are shown. Calculate the height h of the larger tin.

$h =$ .... mm

2 marks

5 A 10 metre high pole is held in place by two metal struts, AE and BC.
The position of the struts is described in the diagram.
AD = 10 m, BC = 6 m, DE = 12 m, AC = 8.5 m
BC is parallel to the level ground DE.
Calculate the length of CE.

CE = ... m

2 marks

9 Units of measurement

French scientists worked out the distance from the North Pole to the Equator and divided by 10 million. They called this distance 1 metre.

Levels 3–5

- **The metric units of length are millimetres (mm), centimetres (cm), metres (m) and kilometres (km).**

  10 mm = 1 cm   100 cm = 1 m   1000 m = 1 km

- **The metric units of capacity are millilitres (ml), centilitres (cl) and litres (l).**

  10 ml = 1 cl   100 cl = 1 l   1000 ml = 1 l

- **The metric units of mass are milligrams (mg), grams (g), kilograms (kg) and tonnes (t).**

  1000 mg = 1 g   1000 g = 1 kg   1000 kg = 1 t

- **To convert between units you need to know the above conversion facts.**

  Convert 4800 g to kilograms.
  Look for the conversion fact that you need.
  To go from the larger unit to the smaller
  unit you multiply.
  To go from the smaller unit to the bigger
  unit you divide.

  > 1000 g = 1 kg
  >
  > g → kg
  > smaller → bigger
  > so divide by 1000

  4800 g ÷ 1000 = 4.8 kg

- **The imperial units of length are inches (in), feet (ft), yards (yd) and miles.**

  12 in = 1 ft   3 ft = 1 yd   1760 yd = 1 mile

- **The imperial units of mass are ounces (oz), pounds (lb) and stones (st).**

  16 oz = 1 lb   14 lb = 1 st

- **The imperial units of capacity are fluid ounces (fl oz), pints (pt) and gallons (gal).**

  20 fl oz = 1 pt   8 pt = 1 gal

- **Converting between metric and imperial units of length.**

  You need to remember these conversion numbers and when to multiply and divide.

	Conversion number
1 in is about 2.5 cm	2.5
1 ft is about 30 cm	30
1 yd is about 90 cm	90
1 mile is about 1.6 km	1.6

  Convert 3 yd to cm
  Look for the conversion number
  that you need.

  $$\text{yd} \rightarrow \text{cm}$$
  $$90$$
  imperial → metric
  so multiply

  3 yds = 3 × 90 = 270 cm

- **Converting mass and capacity.**

	Conversion number
1 oz is about 30 g	30
1 lb is about 450 g	450
1 st is about 6.5 kg	6.5
1 pt is about 600 ml	600
1 gal is about 4.5 l	4.5

- **To read a scale**

  (1) Work out what each division represents.
  (2) Work out the reading.

Each division is 20
The reading is 280

Each division is 0.1
The reading is 7.4

- **Time can be written using am and pm or the 24 hour clock**

morning
7.20 am
07:20

afternoon
5.50 pm
17:50

night
12.15 am
00:15

Level 6

- You need to be able to estimate in both Imperial and metric units.
  Remember these familiar objects to help you.

Length   1 in   1 cm   2 m   6 ft   1 ft   30 cm

Mass   30 g or 1 ounce   1 kg or 2 lb   100 kg or 15 st

Capacity   250 ml or ½ pt   2 l or 3½ pt   90 l or 20 gal

Levels 3–5

1
a 1 m = ... cm
b ...... in = 1 ft
c ...... oz = 1 lb
d 1 kg = ... g

e ...... pt = 1 gal
f 1 l = ... ml
g 2 cm = ... mm
h ...... kg = 3t

i 400 cl = ... l
j ...... oz = 3 lb
k 6 yd = ... ft
l 24 in = ... ft

2
a 1 mile is about ...... km
b 1 pt is about ...... ml

c 1 yd is about ...... cm
d 1 gal is about l

e 1 oz is about ...... g
f 1 lb is about ...... g

3
a

10   20
Each division is ...
The reading is ...

b
5   6
Each division is ...
The reading is ...

c
10   20
Each division is ...
The reading is ...

4
a 6:50 am = ...
b 23:10 = ...

c 01:45 = ...
d 4:36 pm = ...

Level 6

5
a

length is about ...... m

b

mass is about ...... oz

c

width is about ...... in

d

capacity is about ...... ml

Levels 3–5

1

BUS TIMETABLE

Underhill	depart	07:30	08:15	09:00	09:45	10:30
Bramley	arrive	08:05	08:50	09:35	10:20	11:05

a A bus leaves **Underhill** at **09:45**.
At what time does it arrive at **Bramley**? .... 1 mark

b A bus arrives at **Bramley** at **10:20**.
At what time did it leave **Underhill**? .... 1 mark

c How long does the bus journey take from **Underhill** to **Bramley**?

.... minutes 1 mark

d Which buses could you catch to get to **Bramley** by **10:00**?

.... or .... or .... 1 mark

e Vincent needs to be in **Bramley** by **09:00**.
What is the time of the **latest** bus he can catch from **Underhill**?

.... 1 mark

f The last evening bus from
Underhill is at **23:15**.
Draw hands on this clock
face to represent this time.

1 mark

2

a Write down the **length** of the pencil

in centimetres ....   in millimetres .... 2 marks

b Another pencil of length 5.3 cm has 16 mm cut from its length.
What is the new length of the pencil?
Give your answer in centimetres. .... cm 1 mark

3 a A piece of cheese is weighed.
Write down the mass shown
by the scale.

.... kg   1 mark

b 600 g of cheese is cut off.
How much cheese remains?
Give your answer in kilograms.   .... kg   2 marks

Level 6

4 The conversion graph shown on the grid is for centimetres and inches.

a Change **2 inches** into
centimetres.

.... cm

b Change **20 centimetres**
into **inches**.

.... inches

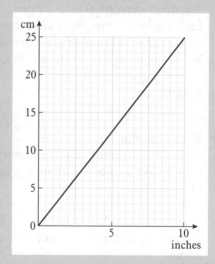

2 marks

5 Write down your estimate of each of the following:

a The mass of a bag of sugar   .... kg

b The capacity of a milk bottle   l

c The length of an ant   .... mm

Level 7

- **Lower and upper limits**
  Any number in the red part of the
  number line rounds to 7 to the nearest
  whole number.

  6.5 is called the lower limit.
  7.5 is called the upper limit.

- $\text{Speed} = \dfrac{\text{Distance}}{\text{Time}}$ $\text{Time} = \dfrac{\text{Distance}}{\text{Speed}}$ $\text{Distance} = \text{Speed} \times \text{Time}$

  This triangle can help you to remember these.
  Cover up the letter you're trying to find.
  What is left is the rest of the equation.

  An object moves 300 m in 2 mins
  Find the average speed in metres per second.
  To get the speed in metres per second you must work in metres and seconds.
  So the object moves 300 m in 120 s.

  $\text{Speed} = \dfrac{300}{120} = 2.5 \text{ m/s}.$

- **Travel graphs**
  The **red** part shows movement away
  from home. 50 km in 2 hours is a speed
  of 25 km/h.
  The **blue** part shows a stop lasting 1 hour.
  The **green** part shows the journey home.
  There is a further 1 hour stop 30 km from
  home.

Distance
from home
(km)

Time (hours)

  The average speed = total distance ÷ total time = $100 \div 6 = 16\frac{2}{3}$ km/h

- $\text{Density} = \dfrac{\text{Mass}}{\text{Volume}}$ $\text{Volume} = \dfrac{\text{Mass}}{\text{Density}}$

  $\text{Mass} = \text{Density} \times \text{Volume}.$

Level 7

1 The sides of this box are correct to the nearest whole number.

6 cm
15 cm
20 cm

   a The lower limits of each length are

   ...... cm, ... cm, ... cm.

   b The upper limits of each length are ...... cm, ... cm, ... cm.

2 The travel graph shows Tim's cycle journey from Cranley to Marsh.

   a How far is it from Cranley to Marsh?

   ....

   b How long did Tim stop for a rest?

   ....

   c Did Tim travel faster before or after his rest? Explain your answer.

   ....

   ....

   d Find Tim's average speed for the whole journey.

   ....

   ....

3 Complete the table.

	Speed	Distance	Time
a		13 m	2 s
b	5 m/s		2.5 mins
c	12 km/h	4 km	
d	mph	40 miles	$1\frac{1}{4}$ hours

4 Complete the table.

	Density	Mass	Volume
a		50 g	10 cm³
b	50 kg/m³	100 kg	
c	15 g/cm³		20 cm³
d	g/cm³	2.5 kg	100 cm³

Levels 5–7

1 Estimate the readings on the following scales.
   Give the units of measurement with your answer.

a ....

b ....

c ....

3 marks

2 The scales show the mass of a man in stones.

a Write down, in **stones and pounds**, the reading on the scales.

.... st .... lb   1 mark

b The man has lost $1\frac{1}{2}$ stones while on a diet.
   How much did the man weigh **before** he went on the diet?

.... st .... lb   1 mark

3 A 600 l tank is being filled with water.
   The table shows some readings taken while the tank is being filled.

Time (min)	1	6	10	15	25	30	
Capacity (litres)		72		180			600

a Complete the table.   2 marks

b C is the capacity of the tank in litres,
   and T is the time in minutes.
   Write an equation using symbols to connect C and T.   ....   1 mark

c A tank of capacity 5000 l is to be filled at the same rate as before.
   How long, in hours and minutes, does it take to fill the tank?

.... hours .... minutes   2 marks

4 Janet exchanges £550 for 154 000 pesetas.

   a Work out the exchange rate.

£1 = ... pesetas   1 mark

   b While on holiday Janet buys a leather
bag for 4600 pesetas.
Work out how much this is in pounds.

£ ....   2 marks

5 The travel graph represents
the journeys of two cyclists,
Adam and Belinda.
Adam is travelling from
Crook to Debens.
Belinda is travelling from
Debens to Crook.

   a How many minutes after Belinda did Adam start his journey?

.... minutes   1 mark

   b Describe briefly what happened at point X.

1 mark

   c Work out the average speed for Adam's entire journey, in kilometres per hour.

.... km/h   1 mark

   d Work out Belinda's average speed using only the amount of time during which
she was actually moving.

.... km/h   1 mark

   e Between which two times was Adam's speed the fastest?

.... and ....   1 mark

10 Perimeter, area and volume

The world record for the number of people in a phone box is 23. This is a lot of people in a very small space!

Levels 3–5

- **The total distance around the outside of a shape is called its perimeter.**
  The perimeter of this shape is
  $5 + 8 + 6 + 10 = 29$ cm

- **Area is measured in squares.**
  The area of this shape is 5 squares.
  If each square is 1 cm by 1 cm then the area is 5 cm².

- **You can count squares to estimate an area.**
  Count all the squares which are more than half inside the outline.
      Area = 10 cm²

- **The area of a rectangle = length × width**
  The area of this rectangle is
      $5 \times 3 = 15$ cm²

- **The area of a triangle** $= \dfrac{\text{base} \times \text{height}}{2}$

  The area of this triangle is
  $\dfrac{6 \times 5}{2} = \dfrac{30}{2} = 15$ cm²

The base and the height must always be at right angles like these.

- **Units of area are always square units.**

- **Volume is measured in cubes.**
  The volume of this solid is 7 cubes.

  If each cube is 1 cm by 1 cm by 1 cm then the volume is 7 cm³.

- **The capacity of a hollow object is the volume of space inside it.**
  Capacity is measured in millilitres and litres. 1 ml is the same as 1 cm³.

Level 6

- **Circumference of a circle = $\pi \times$ diameter**
  The circumference of this circle is $\pi \times 6 = 18.9$ cm (1 dp)

  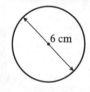
  6 cm

- **Area of a circle = $\pi \times$ radius² = $\pi \times$ radius $\times$ radius**
  The area of this circle is $\pi \times 3 \times 3 = 28.3$ cm² (1 dp)
  The radius is half the diameter.

- **Area of a parallelogram = base $\times$ height**
  The area of this parallelogram is
  $10 \times 7 = 70$ cm²

  height = 7 cm
  base = 10 cm

- **The area of a trapezium $= \dfrac{(a + b)}{2} \times h$**

  You add the two parallel sides, divide by 2 and then multiply by the height.

  a
  h
  b

  The area of this trapezium is
  $\dfrac{(7 + 5)}{2} \times 3 = 6 \times 3 = 18$ cm²

  7 cm
  3 cm
  5 cm

- **Volume of a cuboid = length $\times$ width $\times$ height**
  The volume of this cuboid is
  $8 \times 4 \times 3 = 96$ cm³
  Units of volume are always cube units.

  3 cm
  4 cm
  8 cm

TEST YOURSELF

1 The perimeter of this shape is

...... + ... + ... = ... cm

2 The area of this shape is

...... squares

3 The area of this rectangle is

...... cm × ...... cm = ... cm²

4 The area of this triangle is

$$\frac{...... \times ......}{......} = \frac{......}{......} = ... \text{ cm}^2$$

5 The volume of this solid is

...... cubes

6 The circumference of this circle is

π × ...... = ... cm (1 dp)

The area of this circle is

π × ...... × ...... = ... cm² (1 dp)

7 The area of this trapezium is

$$\frac{(...... + ...)}{......} \times ...... = ... \times ...... = ... \text{ cm}^2$$

8 The volume of this cuboid is

...... × ...... × ...... = ... cm³

Levels 3–5

1 These shapes have been drawn on a 1 cm grid.

Find (i) the perimeter: .... cm   (i) the perimeter: .... cm

(ii) the area: .... cm²   (ii) the area: .... cm²

4 marks

2 How many of the **triangular tiles** can fit inside each shape?

a .... tiles   **b** .... tiles   2 marks

3 This rectangle is made from **six 1 cm square tiles**.

1 mark

The rectangle has an area of **6 cm²** and a perimeter of **10 cm**. Draw another shape which has an area of **6 cm²** but which has a **larger perimeter**.

✓ The tiles must fit
together side to side,
✗ not corner to corner.

4 Work out the **area** of each shape.

a 5 cm, 3 cm   **b** 6 cm, 8 cm   **c** 4 cm, 7 cm

.... cm²   .... cm²   .... cm²

3 marks

5 These shapes are made from small cubes of side 1 cm.
Write down how many small cubes there are in each shape.

a

b

Number of cubes: ....

Number of cubes: ....

2 marks

Level 6

6 **a** This coin has a **diameter** of **12 mm**.
The coin is pushed round exactly **twice**.
Work out how far the coin has moved.

12 mm

.... mm   1 mark

b This coin has a **diameter** of **16 mm**.
The coin has been moved **201 mm**.
How many times has it been pushed round?

16 mm

←— 201 mm —→

.... times   1 mark

7 The area of this square is **9 cm²**.
What is the **perimeter** of the square?

.... cm   1 mark

8 Find the **area** of this parallelogram.

5 cm   4 cm

←—7 cm—→

.... cm²   1 mark

9 The **area** of the trapezium is **24 cm²**.
What is its vertical **height**, h cm?

←—5 cm—→

h cm

←——7 cm——→

.... cm   1 mark

Level 7

- **To find the area of this shape, find the area of the two parts and add them together.**

  Area A = $12 \times 8 = 96$ cm²

  Area B = $\dfrac{\pi \times 4^2}{2} = 25.1$ cm² (1 dp)

  Total area = $96 + 25.1 = 121.1$ cm² (1 dp)

8 cm   A   B

← 12 cm →

- **To find the area of the red shape you have to subtract the areas.**

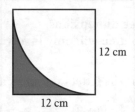

  = $12 \times 12 - \dfrac{\pi \times 12^2}{4}$

  = 144   −   113.1

  = 30.9 cm² (1 dp)

12 cm

12 cm

- **A prism is a solid which is exactly the same shape all the way through.**

  The cross section must be a polygon.

- **Volume of a prism = area of cross section × length**

  The volume of this prism is
  $15 \times 20 = 300$ cm³

15 cm²

20 cm

- **Volume of a cylinder = area of cross section × length**
  = $\pi r^2 \times h$

  The volume of this cylinder is
  $\pi \times 8^2 \times 11 = 2212.0$ cm³ (1 dp)

8 cm

11 cm

- The dimension of a formula is the number of lengths that are multiplied together.

- A constant has no dimension.

- Length has one dimension.
  Formulas for length will only involve constants and lengths.

- Area has two dimensions.
  Formulas for area will only involve constants and length × length.

- Volume has three dimensions.
  Formulas for volume will only involve constants and length × length × length.

In these formulas the letters x, y and x are lengths, k is a constant.

$P = 4xy$ This is constant × length × length
so P is an area.

$Q = \pi y^2 z$ This is constant × length^2 × length
= constant × length × length × length
so Q is a volume.

$R = kx$ This is constant × length
so R is a length.

- If a formula has more than one term, each term must have the same dimension.

$U = cx + \pi y$ Each term has dimension one
so U is a length.

$V = x^2 y - \pi xyz$ Each term has dimension three
so V is a volume.

$W = 2y^2 - 4\pi x$ $2y^2$ has dimension two
$4\pi x$ has dimension one
so W is an incorrect formula for length or area.

Level 7

1 The area of this shape is

$$...... + \frac{...... \times ......}{......}$$

$$= ...... + ... = ... \text{ cm}^2 \text{ (1 dp)}$$

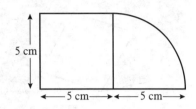

2 The red area is

$$...... - ...... \times ......$$

$$= ...... - ...... = ... \text{ cm}^2 \text{ (1 dp)}$$

3 The volume of this prism is

$$\frac{...... \times ......}{......} \times 15 = ... \text{ cm}^3$$

4 The volume of this cylinder is

$$...... \times ...... \times ......$$

$$= ...... \text{ cm}^3 \text{ (1 dp)}$$

5 The length of this prism is

$$...... \div ...... = ... \text{ cm}$$

Level 8

6 p, q and r are lengths. c and k are constants.
Write 'length', 'area', 'volume' or 'incorrect' for each of these formulas.

$B = cpq$ .... $D = p^2q + 4pqr$ ....

$C = 2kq + \pi r$ .... $E = 4\pi p^2 + ckr$ ....

1

    7 m

    8 m   12 m

  a Calculate the area of the shaded face.

    .... m²   2 marks

  b Calculate the volume of the prism.

    .... m³   1 mark

2

    10 cm

  For this semicircle find:

  a the area   .... cm²   1 mark

  b the perimeter .... cm   1 mark

3 These two triangular prisms have the same cross-sectional area.

What is the height of prism B?

20 cm h cm

Volume A = 100 cm³   Volume B = 60 cm³

Height: .... cm   2 marks

4 This rectangle has a perimeter of **48 cm**.
The length is three times the width.
Calculate the **area** of the rectangle. .... cm² 1 mark

5 A box has internal dimensions as shown.
What is the maximum number of cubes,
of side 2 cm, that can be stacked inside
the cuboid?

2 cm   36 cm   100 cm   50 cm

Number: .... 2 marks

6 Calculate the area of the shaded region.

Area: .... cm²   2 marks

7 Calculate the surface area of this triangular prism.

Area: .... cm²   2 marks

Level 8

8
The surface area of a sphere is calculated using the formula $4\pi r^2$, where r is the radius of the sphere.
This hemisphere has a diameter of 8 cm.
Calculate the total surface area of the entire hemisphere.

Area: .... cm²   3 marks

9 Some of the expressions in the table can be used to calculate lengths, areas or volumes of some shapes.
The letters b, h, l and r represent lengths.
$\pi, 2, 3$, and 4 are numbers which have no dimension.
Put a tick in a box underneath each expression to show whether the expression represents a length, area or volume.

$4\pi r^2$	lbh	$\frac{1}{2}bh$	$\frac{4}{3}\pi r^3$	$4(r+b)$	$\frac{\pi h^2}{b}$	
						Length
						Area
						Volume

2 marks

111

11 Organising data

You can get information from lists of data but graphs and charts show it in a more eye-catching way.

Levels 3–5

- Tally marks are done in groups of five ||||. The total number of tally marks is called the frequency.

- Organise data by making a frequency table.
  This is a frequency table.
  It shows what 30 people have for breakfast.

Breakfast	Tally	Frequency
cereal	|||| |||| ||	12
toast	|||| |||	8
cooked	||||	4
drink only	||||		6

- A pictogram is a diagram which uses pictures to show the data. It must always have a key to show what each picture represents.
  The pictures must all be the same size and in line.
  This pictogram shows the breakfast data.

Cereal

Toast

Cooked

Drinks only

Key: represents 4 people

represents 4 people

so represents 2 people.

- Pictograms are easy to draw except when you need to draw fractions of the picture.

- **A bar chart uses bars instead of pictures to show the frequency.**
  The bars must all be the same width and the same distance apart.
  The heights of the bars are the frequencies. You can add up all the heights to find the total number of people.

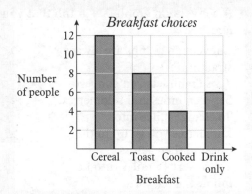

- **You can use a vertical line instead of a bar.**
  This is called a vertical line graph.

- **Instead of a bar chart or vertical line graph you can draw a frequency polygon.**
  The table shows the KS3 Maths results for 30 pupils.

Level	3	4	5	6
Number of pupils	7	8	10	5

Plot the points like coordinates.
Join them up with straight lines.

- **When data is put into groups you can still draw bar charts and frequency polygons.**
  The table shows the percentage test results for 30 pupils.

Score	Number of pupils
50–59	3
60–69	8
70–79	10
80–89	7
90–99	2

The bars in the bar chart now touch.
The red graph is the frequency polygon.
Each point is plotted in the middle of the group.

- **A conversion graph is a graph that you can use to change from one unit to another.**

Conversion graphs are always straight lines.
This graph lets you convert between miles and kilometres.
To change miles into kilometres you go up to the line and then across.
To convert 15 miles into km follow the red lines.
15 miles is 24 km.

To convert 32 km into miles follow the blue lines.
Go across and then down.
32 km is 20 miles.

Conversion graph for distance

- **Another type of diagram is a pie-chart.**
  The angle of the slice represents the frequency.

The pie-chart shows that:
$\frac{1}{2}$ of the chocolates are milk
This is the same as 50%
$\frac{1}{4}$ of the chocolates are plain
This is the same as 25%

If the total number of chocolates is 40

Number of milk chocolates $= \frac{1}{2} \times 40 = 20$
Number of white chocolates $= \frac{1}{4} \times 40 = 10$

Contents of box of chocolates

- **You can only estimate the sizes of the slices for some pie-charts.**

The slice for Fat is a bit more than 25%.
An estimate is 30%.
The slice for Carbohydrate is a bit more than 50%.
An estimate is 60%.

Contents of biscuits

- **All diagrams must be properly labelled and given a title.**

- **Drawing pie-charts**

120 students were asked what they want to do when they leave school.
Here are the results:

Go to university	Go to college	Get a job	Don't know
50	35	25	10

Draw a pie-chart to show this data.

First you need to work out the angles for the pie-chart.
There are 360° to share between the 120 students.
Each student gets 360° ÷ 120 = 3°
Now work out the angle for each slice.

	Number of students	Angle
University	50	$50 \times 3° = 150°$
College	35	$35 \times 3° = 105°$
Job	25	$25 \times 3° = 75°$
Don't know	10	$10 \times 3° = 30°$

Check the angles add up to 360°.
  $150° + 105° + 75° + 30° = 360°$ ✔

You can now draw the pie-chart.

(1) Draw a circle. Mark the centre.
Draw a line to the top of the circle.
Draw the first angle (150°).

(2) Measure the next angle
from the line that you
have just drawn (105°).

(3) Carry on until you have drawn all
the angles.
Label the pie-chart.
You need to label each slice like this.
You also need a title.

*What students
hope to do when
they leave school*

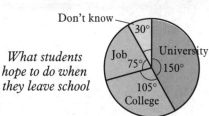

- There are two types of data.
  When data can only take certain individual values it is called discrete data.
  Number of people is discrete data. You can't have 2.8 people.
  When data can have any value it is called continuous data.
  Length, area, mass, time and temperature are all examples of continuous data.

- To draw diagrams for continuous data you must label the horizontal axis as a scale.

Journey times	Number of pupils
5 mins but < 10 mins	5
10 mins but < 15 mins	8
15 mins but < 20 mins	10
20 mins but < 25 mins	7

Time	10:00	12:00	14:00	16:00	18:00	20:00
Temp. (°C)	12	19	20	18	15	10

Bar chart to show journey times

Line graph to show resort temperature

- **Sometimes graphs are used to mislead people.**
  Changing the scale has a big effect.

Graph to show singles sales

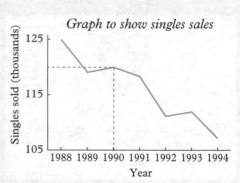

Graph to show singles sales

The two graphs show exactly the same information.
They look very different because of the scales.

1 This data gives you the number of TVs in 30 families.

2 2 3 1 2 3 1 3 2 1 4 2 1 2 2
1 2 2 1 3 2 3 1 3 2 2 4 2 3 1

a Tally these results.

Number of TVs	Tally	Frequency
1		
2		

b Draw a pictogram.
Use to represent two TVs.

Number of TVs

1	
2	
3	
4	

c Draw a bar chart of the data.

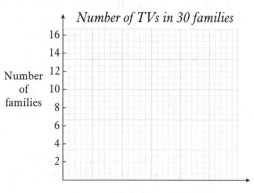

Number of TVs in 30 families

Number of families

16
14
12
10
8
6
4
2

Number of TVs

2 **a** The fraction for gas is ………

b ……% use gas.

c About ……% use storage.

50 households are represented.

d …… households use gas.

Types of heating

Oil

Gas

Storage

Level 6

3 Complete this pie-chart for these sales of hot drinks

Coffee	40
Tea	80
Chocolate	60

Total number of drinks = ………

Each drink gets 360° ÷ …… = ……°

Angle for coffee = ………

Angle for tea = ………

Angle for chocolate = ………

4 Draw a bar chart for this data.

Masses of tomatoes (g)	Frequency
0 to less than 10	6
10 to less than 20	12
20 to less than 30	13
30 to less than 40	4

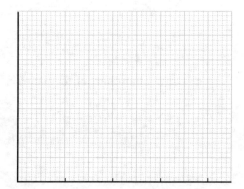

5 This bar chart shows a company's profits in 1995 and 1996. Why is the chart misleading?

……………………………………………

……………………………………………

……………………………………………

……………………………………………

Company profit

Profit (thousands of £)

1 The **pictogram** shows the number of CDs sold on a market stall.
Each symbol represents **4** CDs.

Number of CDs sold

Monday	⊙ ⊙ ⊙ ⊙ ⊙ ⊙ ⊙
Tuesday	⊙ ⊙ ⊙ ⊙ ⊙ (
Wednesday	⊙ ⊙ ⊙ (
Thursday	
Friday	

a How many CDs were sold on

   Monday ....   Tuesday ....   Wednesday ....   3 marks

b CDs were also sold on **Thursday** and **Friday**.
Show these sales figures on the pictogram as symbols.

   9 CDs were sold on Thursday
   24 CDs were sold on Friday.   2 marks

c The market was closed for half a day during the week.
On which day was the market closed for half a day? ....   1 mark

The **following** week a **tally chart** was used to record the sales.

   Monday |||| |||| |||| || Tuesday |||| |||| || Wednesday |||| |||
   Thursday |||| |||| |||| Friday |||| |||| |||| |||

d Give one reason why the **pictogram** is a good way of recording the sales figures.

   ....

   ....   1 mark

e Give one reason why the **tally chart** is a good way of recording the sales figures.

   ....

   ....   1 mark

2 Kim did a survey of **two** types of television programme, on **two** different channels, during a week.

	Channel 1	Channel 3
Films	16	12
Quiz shows	11	13

a How many programmes did Kim record in the week?

.... 1 mark

b What was the **total** number of films shown on **both** channels?

.... 1 mark

c Kim also recorded details of two other types of programme in her survey.

	Mon	Tues	Wed	Thur	Fri
Channel 1	soap, comedy	soap, soap	soap, comedy	soap, comedy	soap, soap, comedy
Channel 3	soap, soap, comedy	soap, soap soap	soap, soap comedy	soap, comedy soap, comedy	soap, comedy comedy

Record this data in the table below.

	Channel 1	Channel 3
Soap		
Comedy		

2 marks

3 Malika did a survey of pets in her class.
She drew a pie-chart to show her results.

a Which pet was the most popular?

....

b Which two pets were equally popular?

.... and ....

Pets in our class

Mice

Fish

Dogs

Cats

Other

Malika recorded **40** pets in her survey.

c How many of the pets were cats? ....

d Estimate how many of the pets were dogs? .... 4 marks

Level 6

4 A surveyor in a street asked people to say which one of five different types of holiday they liked best.
The results are shown below.

Ski	⁙ ⁙ ‖‖‖
Winter abroad	⁙ ⁙ ⁙ ⁙ ⁙ ⁙ ⁙
Summer sun	⁙ ⁙ ⁙ ⁙ ⁙ ⁙ ⁙ ⁙ ⁙ ⁙ ⁙ ⁙ ⁙ ⁙ ⁙ ⁙ ⁙ ⁙ ‖
Touring	⁙ ⁙ ⁙ ⁙ ‖
UK holiday	⁙ ⁙ ⁙ ⁙ ‖‖‖

a Give a reason why this display of the information is **not** clear.

.... 1 mark

b How many people were questioned? .... 1 mark

c Give a reason why a **pie-chart** rather than a **bar chart** is a clearer way to show this information?

.... 1 mark

d Draw a pie-chart to show the holiday information.
Label each section of your pie-chart and give it a title.

3 marks

121

- **Questionnaire design.**

  (1) Questions should not be biased or upset people.

  (2) Questions should be clear and useful to your survey.

  (3) Don't ask questions that give a lot of answers. Structure them so that you can give a choice of possible answers such as

  (a) Yes ☐   No ☐   Don't know ☐

  (b) Agree ☐   Disagree ☐   Don't know ☐

  (c) 0–2 ☐   3–5 ☐   More than 5 ☐

  (d) Strongly agree   1 2 3 4 5   Strongly disagree

- **Frequency polygons can be used to compare two sets of data.**

The red and blue frequency polygons show the exam results of 100 pupils at two schools.

The blue results are higher in general than the red results. This is shown by the blue frequency polygon being generally to the right of the red frequency polygon and being above the red polygon for higher marks.

The red results are more spread out than the blue.

This is shown by the width of each polygon.

T E S T   Y O U R S E L F

Level 7

1 Say what is wrong with each of these questions.

    a Intelligent people watch the TV news. Do you?

    ....

    b How much do you weigh?

    ....

    c What do you think about smoking in restaurants?

    ....

2 50 words are sampled from each of two books and the number of letters in each word counted.

Number of letters	1	2	3	4	5	6	7	8
Number of words, Book A	3	9	14	17	6	1	0	0
Number of words, Book B	4	5	6	10	8	9	5	3

    a Draw a frequency polygon for each book on these axes.

    b Describe the differences between the two books.

    ....

    ....

    ....

    ....

1 Two snack bars keep a record of their sales for a day. The pie charts show the sales of certain items.

Snack bar A: 50 items   *Snack bar B: 100 items*

a Estimate the **percentage** of people in **Snack bar A** who bought a beefburger.

...............%   1 mark

b **100** items were recorded for **Snack bar B**.
Estimate the number of hot dogs that were sold.

....   1 mark

c Explain why the pie-charts do **not** show that more beefburgers were sold in Snack bar A than Snack bar B.

....

....   1 mark

d This table shows the data collected from a third snack bar.

Snack bar C	
Beefburgers	70
Hot dogs	50
Salads	30
Sandwiches	30
Fish	20

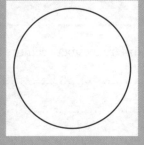

Draw a pie chart to show the information in the table.
Label each section of your pie chart and give it a title.   3 marks

2 Some pupils wanted to find out how much pupils at their school spend on crisps and chocolate. They wrote a questionnaire.

a One of their questions is shown below.
'On average, how much do you spend on crisps and chocolate per day?'

☐	☐	☐	☐	☐	☐
50p or less	5–10p	10–15p	15–20p	20–30p	30p or over

Write down **three** ways in which these boxes could be improved.

....

....

.... 3 marks

b One pupil said, 'We can't give a questionnaire to everyone, so let's just give them to our class to complete.'
Explain what is wrong with this method of collecting the data.

....

....

.... 2 marks

3 The frequency polygon shows the number of TV sets sold by shop assistants Ali and Gary in a shop, over a 10 week period.

a 'It is easy to predict Gary's sales in week 11.' Explain why this statement is true.

.... 1 mark

b 'Ali has the greatest number of sales overall.' Explain why this statement is false.

.... 1 mark

12 Averages

A famous politician once said, 'We want everyone to be better than average.'
You need to understand averages better than he did!

Levels 3–5

- There are three types of average – the mode, the median and the mean.

- The mode is the most common or most popular data value.
  It is sometimes called the modal value.
  The mode is the easiest average to find if there is one.
  The mode of   90 90 95 91 89 91 84 90   is 90

- The median is the middle value when the data is given in order of size.
  To find the median of   29 25 0 32 14 22 14

  (1) Put the numbers in order.   0 14 14 22 25 29 32

  (2) Write down the middle number.   Median = 22

If the number of data values is even you will have two middle numbers. Add these two numbers together and divide by 2 to find the median.
To find the median of   95 91 89 84 90 88

  (1) Put the numbers in order.   84 88 89 90 91 95

  (2) Add the 2 middle numbers and divide by 2.   Median $= \dfrac{89 + 90}{2} = 89.5$

- **To find the mean of a set of data**

  (1) Find the total of all the data values.

  (2) Divide the total by the number of data values.

  To find the mean of   88 90 79 94 86 91

  (1) Add them all up. $88 + 90 + 79 + 94 + 86 + 91 = 528$

  (2) Divide by 6 $528 \div 6 = 88$

  The mean is 88

- **The range of a set of data is the biggest value take away the smallest value.**

  The range of   72 43 62 57 75 63   is $75 - 43 = 32$

  The range is a single number not 43 to 75 or 43−75 which you might see in a newspaper.

  The range tells you how spread out the data is.

- **To compare two sets of data you need**

  (1) A measure of average. This will usually be the mean.

  (2) The range.

  Here are the runs scored by two cricketers in their last 6 innings.

| Ian | 44 | 73 | 39 | 60 | 68 | 40 |
| Gavin | 120 | 7 | 84 | 26 | 9 | 90 |

  Ian's mean is 54 runs. His range is 34 runs.

  Gavin's mean is 56 runs. His range is 113 runs.

  The means are very similar but Gavin's range is much bigger. The bigger range shows that Gavin may score a lot of runs but he may score very few. Ian's smaller range means that he is more consistent.

Level 6

- **You can find averages from frequency tables**

The frequency table shows the number of pit stops in a race.

This row shows that 10 drivers stopped 3 times

Number of stops	Frequency	Stops × Frequency
1	2	1 × 2 = 2
2	11	2 × 11 = 22
3	10	3 × 10 = 30
4	1	4 × 1 = 4
Total = 24		Total = 58

To find the mean add the red column to the table.

$$\text{Mean} = \frac{58}{24} = 2.4 \,(1\,\text{dp})$$

The mode is the number of stops with the highest frequency.

$$\text{Mode} = 2$$

The median is the middle value. The 24 values are

1 1 2 2 2 2 2 2 2 2 2 2 2 3 3 3 3 3 3 3 3 3 4 $\text{Median} = \dfrac{2+2}{2} = 2$

- **A scatter graph is a diagram that is used to see if there is a connection between two sets of data.**

Plot pairs of values like co-ordinates and look for a pattern.

As the height increases so does the weight. This is positive correlation.

As the age increases the value decreases. This is negative correlation.

There is no connection between height and test score. This is zero correlation or no correlation.

- **Correlation can be strong or weak.**

The points lie in a narrow band

Strong positive correlation

The points lie in a wide band

Weak negative correlation

1 24   18   15   21   19   18

    a The mode is ………

    b …………………………

       The median is $\dfrac{…… + ……}{2}$ = ………

    c Total = ………

       Mean = ……… ÷ ………

             = ……… (1 dp)

    d Range = ……… – ……… = ………

2 These are the means and ranges for the times that it takes two taxi companies to get a taxi to a customer.

You have to leave to catch a train in 16 mins. Which company would you call? Explain your answer.

	Mean (min)	Range (min)
Terry's Taxis	12.3	13
Chris' Cabs	12.4	4

....

....

....

3 This table shows the age and sale value of 10 cars.

Age (years)	3	6	5	4	2	6	5	3	6	5
Value (thousands of £)	6.0	2.5	2.9	3.5	6.5	2.3	3.1	5.8	2.1	3.3

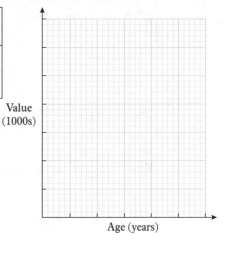

Value (1000s)

Age (years)

    a Draw a scatter graph.
    b The scatter graph shows

      …………………… correlation

      As …………………… increases

      …………………………………

      …………………………………

1   3 4 6 2 1 2 3 5 2 5

   a   Write down the **mode** of this set of numbers.

                                                     .... 1 mark

   b   Write down the **range** of this set of numbers.

                                                     .... 1 mark

   c   Write down the **median** of this set of numbers.

                                                     .... 1 mark

   d   Write down the **mean** of this set of numbers.

                                                     .... 1 mark

2   Over three games Jerry needs to score an average of **12** points to win.
   At his first two attempts he has scored **8** points and **15** points.
   What is the **minimum** number of points he must score in his final game to win?

                                                   .... 2 marks

3   Helen conducts a survey to find the number of pets kept in the homes of pupils. She draws a graph of the results of her survey.

   a   Use the graph to calculate the mean number of pets per pupil.

                                                   .... 1 mark

   b   What is the modal number of pets?

                                                   .... 1 mark

   c   Find the median number of pets.

                                                   .... 1 mark

Level 6

4 A teacher records the number of errors on each test paper marked.
The results are recorded in the table.

Errors	1	2	3	4	5
Frequency	5	6	7	5	3

  a Calculate the **mean** number of errors per pupil.
Show your working.

.... 2 marks

  b Find the **median** number of errors per pupil.

.... 2 marks

  c Explain why the **mean** and the **median** give different values.

....

.... 1 mark

5 The owner of a cafe keeps a record of the number of cups of hot soup, and the
number of cups of coffee that he sells per day, and the temperature on that day.

 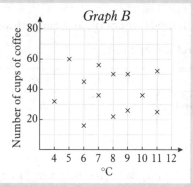

  a What does **graph A** show about the relationship between the number of cups
of hot soup sold, and the temperature on each day.

.... 1 mark

  b What does **graph B** show about the relationship between the number of cups
of coffee sold, and the temperature on each day.

.... 1 mark

- **When a scatter graph shows correlation the points will look as though they lie around a straight line. This line is called the line of best fit. You can use this line to estimate values.**

This scatter graph shows weights and heights of 6-month-old babies.

The red line is the line of best fit. You draw this with a ruler. Try to have about the same number of points on each side of the line.

To estimate the weight for a height of 65 cm draw the blue lines and read off the answer **6.8** kg.

To estimate the height for a weight of 6 kg draw the green lines and read off the answer **62** cm.

- **Finding mean, mode, median, and range for grouped data.**

Here are the results of a test.

Mark	31–40	41–50	51–60	61–70	71–80	81–90	91–100
Number of pupils	5	14	28	35	24	16	8

Look at the first column of data.

You can see that 5 pupils scored between 31 and 40 but you do not know exactly what each of them scored.

To work out an **estimate** for the mean you have to assume that all 5 of them scored the middle mark of the group.

This middle mark is $\dfrac{31 + 40}{2} = 35.5$

You can work out all the mid-points and show these in a new table.

Mark	35.5	45.5	55.5	65.5	75.5	85.5	95.5
Number of pupils	5	14	28	35	24	16	8

You can now **estimate** the mean as

$$\frac{35.5 \times 5 + 45.5 \times 14 + 55.5 \times 28 + 65.5 \times 35 + 75.5 \times 24 + 85.5 \times 16 + 95.5 \times 8}{5 + 14 + 28 + 35 + 24 + 16 + 8}$$

$$= \frac{8605}{130} = 66.2 \text{ marks (1 dp)}.$$

- **When data is grouped you cannot tell which data value is the most common. You can only say which group has the highest frequency. This group is called the modal group.**

  For the test results the modal group is 61–70 marks.

- **When data is grouped you can only say which group the median is in.**

  For the 130 test results the median would be the $\dfrac{65^{\text{th}} + 66^{\text{th}}}{2}$ data value.

  The 65th and 66th values lie in the group 61–70 because the first 3 groups contain 47 data values and the first 4 groups contain 82 data values.

  The median is in the 61–70 group.

- **An estimate for the range is the biggest possible value take away the smallest possible value.**

  For the test marks an **estimate** for the range is

  $100 - 31 = 69$ marks.

- **Cumulative frequency is a running total.**
  This table shows the lifetimes, in hours, of 375 light bulbs.

The red part of the table is a cumulative frequency table. The red lifetime column shows the upper end of each class.

Lifetime	Frequency	Lifetime	Cumulative frequency
201–400	56	400 or less	56
401–600	124	600 or less	180
601–800	101	800 or less	281
801–1000	63	1000 or less	344
1001–1200	31	1200 or less	375

It is often useful to draw a curve from a cumulative frequency table.

The graph is called a **cumulative frequency curve**.
It allows you to estimate cumulative frequencies for points that are not at the ends of the groups.

A cumulative frequency curve is drawn with the values on the horizontal axis and the cumulative frequency on the vertical axis.
The points are always plotted at the **end** of each range.
The points are joined with a smooth curve.

If you are asked to draw a cumulative frequency diagram you can join the points with straight lines instead of a curve.

Cumulative frequency curve to show bulb lifetimes

Notice how the curve is joined back to the beginning of the first range in the original table. This is the point (200, 0).

To estimate the number of bulbs that lasted less than 700 hours:
(1) Draw the red line up from 700 on the horizontal axis to the curve and then across to the vertical axis.
(2) Read the value from this axis.
In this example this is approximately 220 bulbs.

- **The median is the middle data value.**

  To get an estimate of the median:
  (1) Find half the total frequency on the cumulative frequency axis.
  (2) Draw a line across to the curve.
  (3) Draw down to the horizontal axis.
  (4) Read off the estimate of the median.

- **The lower quartile is the value one quarter of the way through the data values.**

  To find the lower quartile:
  (1) Find one quarter of the total frequency on the cumulative frequency axis.
  (2) Draw lines as you did for the median.

- **The upper quartile is the value three quarters of the way through the data.**

- **The interquartile range is the difference between the upper quartile and the lower quartile. This tells you how spread out the central half of the data is.**

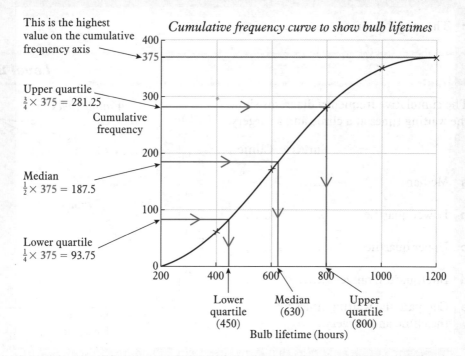

Cumulative frequency curve to show bulb lifetimes

Median = 630 Lower quartile = 450 Upper quartile = 800
Interquartile range = 800 − 450 = 350

- **You can use the median and the interquartile range to compare two sets of data.**

T E S T   Y O U R S E L F

1 The table show the wages of people who work in a car factory.

Wages, £000s	1–10	11–20	21–30	31–100
Wages, mid-points	......	......	......	......
Number of people	25	39	10	6

a Fill in the mid-points in the table.

b Estimate of mean wage $= \dfrac{\ldots\ldots \times \ldots\ldots + \ldots\ldots \times \ldots\ldots + \ldots\ldots \times \ldots\ldots + \ldots\ldots \times \ldots\ldots}{\ldots\ldots + \ldots\ldots + \ldots\ldots + \ldots\ldots}$

$= \dfrac{\ldots\ldots}{\ldots\ldots} = \ldots\ldots$ to nearest £1000

c The modal group is ....

2 The cumulative frequency diagrams show the waiting times at a clinic and a surgery.

Waiting times

               Surgery Clinic

a Median   ....

b Lower quartile   ....

c Upper quartile   ....

d Interquartile range ....

e Compare the waiting times for the clinic and surgery.

....

....

....

1 Barry is doing a geography project.

He records on a graph the number of hours of clear sky on certain days, and the temperature at a certain time on these days.

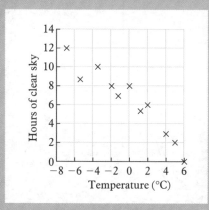

a What does the graph show about the relationship between the hours of clear sky and the temperature in °C?

....

....

....

.... 1 mark

b Draw a **line of best fit** on the scatter diagram. 2 marks

Use your line to find an estimate of the hours of clear sky when the temperature is **2°C**.

.... hours 1 mark

Use your line to find an estimate of the temperature on a day when there are **4 hours of clear sky**.

............°C 1 mark

137

2 Kim counts the number of paces between each of the houses on her paper round.
She groups and records the information in a table.

Number of paces	Midpoint (x)	Frequency (f)	fx
30–39	34.5	3	105
40–49	44.5	8	
50–59	54.5	11	
60–69	64.5	9	
70–79	74.5	13	
80–89	84.5	6	
Totals		50	

a Calculate an estimate of the **mean** number of paces per house.

.... 2 marks

b Write down the group within which the **median** will lie.

.... 1 mark

3 The cumulative frequency graph shows the distribution of ages for 200 people in a village.

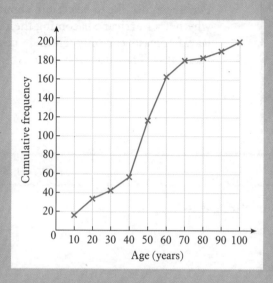

a Use the graph to estimate the **median** age of the people in the village.

.... years   1 mark

b Use the graph to estimate the **interquartile range** of the ages.

.... years   2 marks

c Estimate the **percentage** of the village population who are under 50 years of age.

.... %   1 mark

13 Probability

People would like to be certain about whether a hurricane is coming their way. Forecasts can only tell them how likely it is. They use probabilities.

Levels 3–5

- **Probability tells you how likely something is to happen.**
- **You can show probabilities on a scale.**

The scale shows the probabilities that
(a) a newly born baby will be a girl
(b) you will live to be 300
(c) the next person to come into the room will be right handed.

- **You can use probability to decide whether something is fair or not.**
This spinner is being used by two friends to see who eats the last Rolo.
One person eats it if the spinner lands on blue, the other person eats it if the spinner lands on yellow.
This is not fair. There is a greater chance that the spinner will land on blue. If you spin it 4 times you would expect to get 3 blues and 1 yellow.

- **Probability is written as a number between 0 and 1.**
You can only use fractions, decimals, or percentages to show probabilities.

- **Events are equally likely if they have the same chance of happening.**

  You can use equally likely events to work out probabilities.

  100 tickets are sold for a raffle.
  The probability that you will win if you have 1 ticket is $\frac{1}{100}$.

  The probability that you will win if you have 5 tickets is $\frac{5}{100}$ because each of the tickets is equally likely to win.

- **There are three methods for working out probabilities.**

  (1) Use equally likely outcomes.
      The probability of getting a 4 with a fair dice is $\frac{1}{6}$

  (2) Use a survey or do an experiment.
      If the events are not equally likely you need to do a survey or experiment to see which is more likely.

  (3) Look back at data.
      If the events are not equally likely and you can't do an experiment, then you look back at data. To find the probability that it will snow in London on Christmas Day look back at the records to see how likely it is.

Level 6

- **Probabilities must add up to 1.**
  If the probability of rain is 0.4 then the probability of no rain is $1 - 0.4 = 0.6$

- **A sample space is a list of all the possible outcomes.**
  A table showing these is called a **sample space diagram**.

  The sample space diagram for the possible outcomes of using this spinner and coin is

		Spinner		
		1	2	3
Coin	H	H, 1	H, 2	H, 3
	T	T, 1	T, 2	T, 3

The probability of getting a tail and an odd number $= \frac{2}{6} = \frac{1}{3}$

141

TEST YOURSELF

1 Mark these probabilities.

   a The Sun will rise tomorrow.

   b Ice will be found on the Sun.

   c The Sun will shine on the first day of spring.

```
├─────────────┼─────────────┤
0            0.5            1
```

2 Sue puts these counters into a bag.
   She picks a counter at random.

   a What colour is she more likely to get? ....

   b What is the probability that she will get a blue counter? ....

   c Sue picks out a counter and replaces it. She does this 16 times.

      How many red counters does she expect to get? ....

   d She wants to make it equally likely that she will get a red or a blue counter.

      What extra counters does she need to put in the bag? ....

3 Choose the method to find each probability.

Method 1   Use equally likely outcomes.
Method 2   Use a survey or do an experiment.
Method 3   Look back at data.

   a The next car passing will be red.   Method ......

   b You will get an even number when you roll a fair dice.   Method ......

   c There will be an earthquake somewhere in the world today.   Method ......

4 a Fill in the sample space diagram.

		Dice					
		1	2	3	4	5	6
Coin	H				H, 4		
	T						

   b Find the probability of getting a head and an even number. ....

   c Write down the probability of not getting a head and an even number. ....

PRACTICE QUESTIONS

1 A box contains cubes which are **five** different colours –

red, green, blue, orange and brown.

There are the same number of cubes of each colour in the box.
Bill takes a cube out of the box without looking.

a What is the **probability** that Bill will get a **red** or a **blue** cube?

.... 1 mark

b What is the **probability** that Bill will get a **yellow** cube?

.... 1 mark

c Draw a cross on the probability scale to show the probability that Bill will get a **blue** or a **brown** cube.

```
|--+--+--+--+--+--+--+--+--+--|
0                             1
```

.... 1 mark

d Draw a cross on the probability scale to show the probability that Bill will **not** get a **green** cube.

```
|--+--+--+--+--+--+--+--+--+--|
0                             1
```

.... 1 mark

2 This wheel is spun around.
It will stop with the arrow
pointing at a colour.

a Liam says that **red** is more likely than any other colour.
Explain why Liam is **wrong**.

....

....

.... 1 mark

b The wheel is spun, and stops with the arrow pointing at **yellow**.
What is the **probability** that the wheel will stop on the **yellow** when it is spun again?

.... 1 mark

143

c Colour or shade this spinner so that it will be **certain** that the arrow will land on the **same colour** each time.

1 mark

d Colour or shade this spinner so that there is a **0.5 chance** the spinner will land on **one colour**.

1 mark

3 A coin is thrown and lands on heads **four** times in a row.

a Draw a cross on the probability scale to show the probability of it landing on heads on the **fifth** throw.

```
├──┼──┼──┼──┼──┼──┼──┼──┼──┼──┤
0                              1
```

1 mark

b **Two** coins are thrown together.
What is the probability that you will throw two heads together?

.... 1 mark

c What is the probability that you will **not** throw two tails with two coins?

.... 1 mark

Level 6

4 Julie has a bag containing 20 coloured counters.
She takes 4 red counters out of the bag without looking.

a Julie says, 'The bag must only contain red counters.'
Explain why Julie may be **wrong**.

....

.... 1 mark

b Julie then takes out two blue and one green counter.
She says, 'As I have 4 red, 2 blue and 1 green counter then the probability in the future of me picking a red is $\frac{4}{7}$, picking a blue is $\frac{2}{7}$, and a green $\frac{1}{7}$.'
Explain why Julie is **wrong**.

....

....

.... 1 mark

Level 7

- **The frequency of an event is the number of times that it happens.**

- **The relative frequency of an event** $= \dfrac{\text{frequency of the event}}{\text{total frequency}}$

The relative frequency gives an estimate of the probability.
This estimate can be improved by increasing the number of times the experiment is repeated.

A drawing pin is dropped 100 times.
It lands point up or point down.
The table shows the results.

The relative frequency of up $= \frac{67}{100}$

$= 0.67$

Position	Frequency
up	67
down	33

An estimate of the probability that the drawing pin will land point up is 0.67
This estimate will get closer to the true probability as the pin is dropped more times.

Level 8

- **Events are mutually exclusive if they cannot happen at the same time.**

When a coin is thrown it can land showing either a head or a tail. It cannot show a head and a tail at the same time. They are mutually exclusive events.
When a playing card is chosen from a pack getting an ace and getting a heart are not mutually exclusive. The ace of hearts satisfies both events.

- When combining mutually exclusive events you add the probabilities

  $P\,(\text{diamond}) = \frac{1}{4}$ $P\,(\text{club}) = \frac{1}{4}$
  $P\,(\text{diamond or club}) = \frac{1}{4} + \frac{1}{4} = \frac{1}{2}$

- The word '**or**' means **add** the probabilities.

145

- **Two events are independent if the outcome of one has no effect on the outcome of the other.**

  When you roll a dice and throw a coin the outcome from the dice has no effect on the outcome of the coin. These are independent events.

- **When combining independent events you multiply the probabilities.**

  P (getting a 4 on a dice) $= \frac{1}{6}$ P (getting head on a coin) $= \frac{1}{2}$
  P (getting a 4 **and** a head) $= \frac{1}{6} \times \frac{1}{2} = \frac{1}{12}$

- The word '**and**' means **multiply** the probabilities.
  Watch for other words like '**both**' being used instead of 'and'.

- **You can use tree diagrams to show the outcomes of more than one event.**

  This is a tree diagram for throwing two dice when you want to know how many 6s you get.

  P (getting two 6s) $= \frac{1}{6} \times \frac{1}{6} = \frac{1}{36}$

  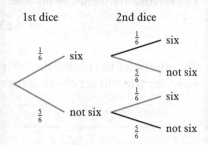

  'Getting two 6s' is the same as 'getting a 6 **and** getting a 6'.
  This is also the same as 'getting a 6 on **both** dice'
  The probability of only getting one 6 is shown by the green routes through the tree.

  P (getting one 6) $=$ P(6 **and** not 6) **or** P (not 6 **and** 6)
  $\qquad = \frac{1}{6} \times \frac{5}{6} \;+\; \frac{5}{6} \times \frac{1}{6}$
  $\qquad = \frac{10}{36}$
  $\qquad = \frac{5}{18}$

- **You multiply the probabilities along the branches. You add the probabilities if you use more than one route.**

Level 7

1 The table shows the colours of cars passing a school.

Colour	Frequency
black	8
red	35
white	28
other	29

a The total number of cars = ...

b Relative frequency of black = ...

c An estimate of the probability that the next car to pass the school will be red = ...

d How can the estimate in **c** be made more accurate?

....

Level 8

2 These two dice are thrown.
Find the probability that

a the red dice will show a 3 or a 5 ....

b the red dice will show a 3 and the green dice will show an even number ....

c both dice will show a 6 ....

3 The probability that a pupil has chips for lunch is 0.6

a Fill in the tree diagram to show the choices of the next 2 pupils.

Use the tree diagram to find the probability that

b the next 2 pupils both have chips

....

c only one of the next 2 pupils has chips

....

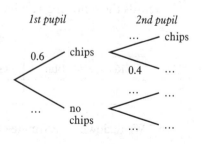

1st pupil   *2nd pupil*

0.6 — chips ... chips

0.4 ...

... — no chips

...

...

...

Levels 5–7

1 Amanda and Gurjeet each have a spinner.
They **add** the scores on their spinners.

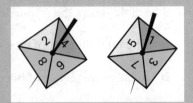

a Complete the table below to show all their possible answers.

+	2	4	6	8
1				
3				
5				
7				

1 mark

b What is the **probability** that their answer is a number **greater than 9**?

.... 1 mark

c What is the **probability** that their answer is a number which is a **square number**?

.... 1 mark

d What is the **probability** that their answer is an **even** number?

.... 1 mark

2 This **biased** cube has coloured faces.
Tony throws the cube **60** times, and
records the following results.

Red	Blue	Green	Yellow	Orange	Purple
30	5	6	8	7	4

a Write down an estimate of the probability of throwing a **red** with this cube.

.... 1 mark

b How many times would you expect to get a red if you threw the cube **20 times**?

.... 1 mark

c Tony threw the cube **20 times**, but only got a red on **4** occasions.
Can you explain this?

....

.... 1 mark

d How could Tony improve the accuracy of his results?

....

.... 1 mark

Level 8

3 A road traffic survey showed that the probability of a car having to stop at a traffic light is **0.7**
On a particular road there are two sets of traffic lights.

a Calculate the probability that a car will pass through **both** sets of traffic lights without having to stop.

.... 1 mark

b Calculate the probability that a car will be stopped at **only one** of the sets of traffic lights as it passes along the road.

.... 2 marks

c Karen passes through the traffic lights **80 times** in a month.
How many times during the month should she expect to be stopped at the **first set** of traffic lights?

.... 1 mark

1 Whole numbers

Levels 3–5 (p. 8)

1 a 30   **b** 100

2 a 28   **b** 54   **c** 3

3 a 260   **b** 4100   **c** 10

4 a 36   **b** 80   **c** 10

5 a
```
   260
 +123
  383
```
c
```
  174
 - 51
  123
```

b
```
  187
 + 35
  222
   11
```
d
```
  2⁶7¹1
 -  46
   225
```

6 a
```
    237
 ×   25
   1185
   4740
   5925
      1
```
b
```
     23
 14)32⁴2

 1 × 14 = 14
 2 × 14 = 28
 3 × 14 = 42
```

7 $-6, -4, 0, 5, 12$

8 3 °C

Level 6 (p. 8)

9 a 10   **d** -5 **g** -3

  b -11 **e** 20   **h** 6

  c 28   **f** -18 **i** 50

Level 7 (p. 13)

1 a ÷   **b** ×   **c** ×   **d** ÷

2 a

`( 4 . 8 6 × 1 . 6 3 ) ÷`
`( 4 . 3 7 + 1 . 9 4 ) =`

b

`( 4 . 2 + 3 . 6 x² ) ÷`
`( 4 . 9 1 − 2 . 8 7 ) =`

Level 8 (p. 13)

3 a 625   **b** 9   **c** 3   **d** 64

4 a 5×10^{-3} **b** 1.2×10^{7}

5 a 281 000   **b** 0.000 000 83

6 a

`4 . 2 EXP 6 ÷ 2 . 1 EXP`
`4 ⁺⁄₋ =`

2 Fractions, decimals and percentages

Levels 3–5 (p. 21)

1 a
```
   2.14
 +1.79
  3.93
    1
```
c
```
    2.53
 ×    24
  10.12
  50.60
  60.72
```

b
```
  1¹2.⁶7¹6
 -   8.58
    4.18
```
d
```
    1.79
 5)8.³9⁴5
```

2 a $224 \div 8 = 28$

    $28 \times 5 = £140$

  b $900 \div 100 = 9$

    $9 \times 72 = 648$ g

3 a   **b**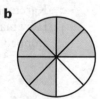

TEST YOURSELF ANSWERS

Level 6 (p. 21)

4

Fraction	$\frac{1}{2}$	$\frac{1}{4}$	$\frac{1}{5}$	$\frac{3}{4}$	$\frac{3}{5}$	$\frac{81}{100}$
Decimal	0.5	0.25	0.2	0.75	0.6	0.81
Percentage	50%	25%	20%	75%	60%	81%

5 a $\frac{16}{40} = \frac{2}{5}$

b 35 p as a percentage of 250 p

$= \frac{35}{250} \times 100\% = 14\%$

6 Total number of parts = 9
Value of 1 part = 180 ÷ 9 = £20
Value of each share
2 × £20 = £40   3 × £20 = £60
4 × £20 = £80

Level 7 (p. 25)

1 a 20% of 650 g = 130 g
New amount = 780 g
b $\frac{2}{5}$ of £460 = £184
New amount = £644

2 a 15% of 370 cm = 55.5 cm
New amount = 314.5 cm
b $\frac{3}{8}$ of 2400 kg = 900 kg
New amount = 1500 kg

3 17.5% of 60 = £10.50
Total bill = £70.50

Level 8 (p. 25)

4 Year 1
15% of £8600 = £1290
New value = 8600 − 1290 = £7310
Year 2
15% of £7310 = £1096.50
New value = 7310 − 1096.50 = £6213.50

Year 3
15% of £6213.50 = £932.03
New value = 6213.50 − 932.03
= £5281.47

5 100% + 7% = 107%
1% = 2568 ÷ 107 = 24
100% = 24 × 100 = 2400

6 $\frac{3}{17}$ is 420 so $\frac{1}{17}$ is 140
Number of people now is
140 × 17 = 2380

3 Estimating

Levels 3–5 (p. 30)

1 a 15 + 3
= 18
b 26 − 15
= 11
c 24 − 4
= 20
d 7 × 4
= 28
e 14 ÷ 2 + 7
= 7 + 7 = 14
f 9 + 24
= 33

2 a 2   **c** 140   **e** 100
b 50   **d** 400

3 a 34 × 176 = 5984
34 = 30 to the nearest 10
176 = 200 to the nearest 100
30 × 200 = 6000
b 858 ÷ 33 = 26
858 = 900 to the nearest 100
33 = 30 to the nearest 10
900 ÷ 30 = 30

Level 6 (p. 30)

4 a 7.9   **c** 13.4   **e** 4.857
b 6.32   **d** 29.09   **f** 4.70

5 1 tape costs £11.50 ÷ 8 = £1.44

Level 7 (p. 33)

1 **a** 4 **c** 30 **e** 7000
b 0.07 **d** 0.007 **f** 10 000

2 **a** 500 000 **f** 150
b 24 000 **g** 300
c 0.0003 **h** 20
d 0.000 42 **i** 7000
e 80 **j** 30 000

3 **a** $\dfrac{40 \times 10}{2}$ **b** $\dfrac{40 \times 50}{10 \times 20}$

$= \dfrac{400}{2}$ $= \dfrac{2000}{200}$

$= 200$ $= 10$

Level 8 (p. 33)

4 **a** $\sqrt{17} \approx \sqrt{16} = 4$ **b** $\sqrt{87} \approx \sqrt{81} = 9$

5 $\sqrt{\dfrac{25 \times 64}{16}} \approx \sqrt{\dfrac{30 \times 60}{20}} = \sqrt{\dfrac{1800}{20}}$

$= \sqrt{90} \approx \sqrt{81} = 9$

4 Patterns and sequences

Levels 3–5 (p. 38)

1 **a** 7, 21, 42 **c** 1, 3, 10, 21
b 2, 3, 7, 13, 23 **d** 1, 8, 64

2 **a** 4, 8, 12, 16, 20, 24, 28, 32, 36, 40
b 9, 18, 27, 36, 45, 54, 63, 72, 81, 90
c 36

3 **a** 36 **b** 49 **c** 10 **d** 8

Level 6 (p. 38)

4 **a** add 5 **c** $3 + 49 \times 5 = 248$
b 5 **d** $5n - 2$

Level 7 (p. 42)

1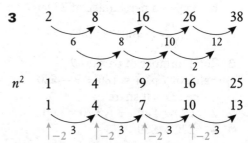

The formula is $7n - 3$

2 **a** $4 \times 1 - 3 = 1$
b $4 \times 6 - 3 = 21$
c $4 \times 20 - 3 = 77$

3

The formula is $n^2 + 3n - 2$

4 **a** $3 - 1 - 2 = 0$
b $3 \times 25 - 5 - 2 = 68$

5 Formulas and equations

Levels 3–5 (p. 47)

1 **a** $c = 25 + 15h$
b $25 + 15 \times 4 = £85$

2 $P = 2l + 2w$

Level 6 (p. 47)

3

Value of x	Value of $4x^2 - 27$	
10	$4 \times 10^2 - 27 = 373$	too small
20	$4 \times 20^2 - 27 = 1573$	too big
22	$4 \times 22^2 - 27 = 1909$	too small
21	$4 \times 21^2 - 27 = 1737$	correct

$x = 21$

4 a $x + 7 - 7 = 13 - 7$
$x = 6$

b $\dfrac{x}{6} - 3 + 3 = 4 + 3$
$\dfrac{x}{6} = 7$
$\dfrac{x}{6} \times 6 = 7 \times 6$
$x = 42$

c $5x - x - 28 = x - x - 6$
$4x - 28 = -6$
$4x = 22$
$x = 5.5$

d $x - 3 = 7$
$x = 10$

Level 7 (p. 53)

1 a $2x \leqslant 8$
$x \leqslant 4$

b $\dfrac{x}{5} > 3$
$x > 15$

2 $0, 1, 2, 3, 4$

Level 8 (p. 53)

3 a $x \geqslant 0$
b $y \leqslant x + 3$
c $-4 < y \leqslant 4$

4 a $x + c^2 = 2r$
$r = \dfrac{x + c^2}{2}$
b $\sqrt{p} \leqslant r - s$
$r = \sqrt{p} + s$

5 a $2(7q - 4)$
b $8a(2a^2 - 1)$

6 a $x^2 - 3x + 4x - 12 = x^2 + x - 12$
b $2x^2 - 12x - 3x + 18 = 2x^2 - 15x + 18$

6 Functions and graphs

Levels 3–5 (p. 58)

1 A $(4, 2)$ B $(1, 4)$ C $(0, 2)$

2

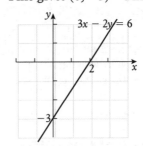

Level 6 (p. 58)

3 $y = x + 2$

4 A $x = 2$ C $y = -x$
   B $y = 2x + 2$ D $y = -x - 3$

5 When $x = 0$ When $y = 0$
    $-2y = 6$ $3x = 6$
    $y = -3$ $x = 2$
This gives $(0, -3)$ This gives $(2, 0)$

Level 7 (p. 65)

1 a Adding gives $5x = 20$
                          $x = 4$
  Put $x = 4$ into (1)
                $2 \times 4 + y = 14$
                          $y = 6$
  Solution is $x = 4, y = 6$
  Check in (2)
    $3 \times 4 - 6 = 12 - 6 = 6$ ✓

b Multiply (1) by 3 and (2) by 2
$$12x + 6y = 30$$
$$10x + 6y = 24$$
Subtracting $\quad 2x = 6$
$$x = 3$$
Put $x = 3$ into (1)
$$4 \times 3 + 2y = 10$$
$$y = -1$$
The solution is $x = 3, y = -1$
Check in (2) $5 \times 3 + 3 \times -1 = 12$ ✓

Level 8 (p. 65)

2 A $\quad y = x^2 - 4x + 7$

B $\quad y = \dfrac{1}{x - 3}$

C $\quad y = x^3 - 6x^2 + 11x - 6$
D $\quad y = 4 - x^2$

3

Height increases slowly at first but then rate of increase gets bigger. Then constant rate of increase for the last part.

7 2D and 3D shapes

Levels 3–5 (p. 72)

1 a obtuse   **b** acute   **c** reflex

2 a W   **b** SE   **c** E   **d** NE

3 a $70 + 110 = 180$ $110°$
  b $35 + 55 + 90 = 180$ $55°$
  c $80 + 20 + 80 = 180$ $80°$

Level 6 (p. 72)

4 a   **b**   **c**

5 a $90 + 90 + 40 + 80 = 300$
$360 - 300 = 60°$
  b $40 + 140 = 180$ **140°**

6 a Angles on straight line
$130 + 50 = 180$ **50°**
  b Opposite angles   **80°**
  c Angles in triangle
$50 + 80 + 50 = 180$ **50°**

Level 7 (p. 77)

1 a $x^2 = 8^2 + 13^2$
$\qquad = 233$
$\quad x = \sqrt{233}$
$\quad x = 15.3$ (3 sf)

  b $\qquad 12.3^2 = x^2 + 7.8^2$
$12.3^2 - 7.8^2 = x^2$
$\qquad\qquad x^2 = 90.45$
$\qquad\qquad x = \sqrt{90.45} = 9.51$ (3 sf)

Level 8 (p. 77)

2 a $\tan 38 = \dfrac{p}{14.1}$

$14.1 \times \tan 38 = p$
$p = 11.0$ cm (3 sf)

  b $\cos p = \dfrac{11}{17}$

$p = 49.7°$ (3 sf)

3 $\sin 54 = \dfrac{x}{500}$

$x = 500 \times \sin 54$
$\quad = 405$ miles (3 sf)

8 Position and movement

Levels 3–5 (p. 84)

1 a

order 3

c

order 4

b

order 2

d

order 3

2

2 a

b

3 The region is shaded.
The boundaries are not included.

Scale: 1 cm to 2 km

Hospital

Motorway

Level 6 (p. 84)

3

C•

4 a 2   **b** 1   **c** 4

Level 7 (p. 89)

1

C•

Level 8 (p. 89)

4 a

P

10 cm

S

R

Q   7 cm   4 cm

T

b (1) ST   (2) QR

c $10 \div 4 = 2.5$ (or $2\frac{1}{2}$)

d $7 \div 2.5 = 2.8$ cm

9 Units of measurement

Levels 3–5 (p. 95)

1
a 100 e 8 i 4
b 12 f 1000 j 48
c 16 g 20 k 18
d 1000 h 3000 l 2

2
a 1.6 c 90 e 30
b 600 d 4.5 f 450

3
a 2, 18 b 0.1, 5.6 c 2, 13

4
a 06:50 c 1:45 am
b 11:10 pm d 16:36

5
a Any in range 3 to 6 m.
b Any in range 3 to 8 oz.
c Any in range 2 to 4 in.
d Any in range 30 to 100 ml.

Level 7 (p. 99)

1
a 19.5 cm, 14.5 cm, 5.5 cm
b 20.5 cm, 15.5 cm, 6.5 cm

2
a 60 km b $1\frac{1}{2}$ hours
c After. The gradient is steeper after his rest.
Speed before = $20 \div 1\frac{1}{2} = 13\frac{1}{3}$ km/h
Speed after = $40 \div 2 = 20$ km/h
d $60 \div 5 = 12$ km/h

3
a $13 \div 2 = 6.5$ m/s
b $5 \times (2.5 \times 60) \div 750$ m
c $4 \div 12 = \frac{1}{3}$ h = 20 mins
d $40 \div 1\frac{1}{4} = 32$ mph

4
a $50 \div 10 = 5$ g/cm^3
b $100 \div 50 = 2$ m^3
c $15 \times 20 = 300$ g
d $(2.5 \times 1000) \div 100 = 25$ g/cm^3

10 Perimeter, area and volume

Levels 3–5 (p. 104)

1 $12 + 9 + 5 = 26$ cm

2 6 squares

3 $11 \times 3 = 33$ cm^2

4 $\dfrac{4 \times 10}{2} = \dfrac{40}{2} = 20$ cm^2

5 6 cubes

Level 6 (p. 104)

6 $\pi \times 16 = 50.3$ cm (1 dp)
$\pi \times 8 \times 8 = 201.1$ cm^2 (1 dp)

7 $\dfrac{(8 \times 10)}{2} \times 6 = 9 \times 6 = 54$ cm^2

8 $6 \times 8 \times 10 = 480$ cm^3

Level 7 (p. 109)

1 $25 + \dfrac{(\pi \times 5^2)}{4}$
$= 25 + 19.6349 \ldots$
$= 44.6$ cm^2 (1 dp)

2 $36 - \pi \times 3^2$
$= 36 - 28.2743 \ldots$
$= 7.7$ cm^2 (1 dp)

3 $\dfrac{6 \times 7}{2} \times 15 = 315$ cm^3

4 $\pi \times 7^2 \times 5 = 769.7$ cm^3 (1 dp)

5 $150 \div 25 = 6$ cm

Level 8 (p. 109)

6 B Area D Volume
C Length E Incorrect

11 Organising data

Levels 3–5 (p. 117)

1 a

Number of TVs	Tally	Frequency
1										8
2															13
3									7
4				2

b *Number of TVs*

1
2
3
4

c *Number of TVs in 30 families*

Number of families

Number of TVs

2 a $\frac{1}{2}$ **b** 50% **c** 20% **d** 25

Level 6 (p. 118)

3 Total number of drinks = 180
Each drink gets 360 ÷ 180 = 2°
Angle for coffee = 80°
Angle for tea = 160°
Angle for chocolate = 120°

Sales of hot drinks

Coffee
Chocolate
Tea

4

Masses of tomatoes

Frequency

Masses of tomatoes (g)

5 Chart is misleading because the bar
for 1996 is twice as wide as the 1995
bar. The area is affected by more than
the change in profits and the eye will
register the area rather than just the
height.

Level 7 (p. 123)

1 a Biased because people will answer
Yes as they want to appear
intelligent.
b There will be a wide variety of
answers – they could well be all
different.

157

c People will give opinions and these will be impossible to analyse properly.

2 a

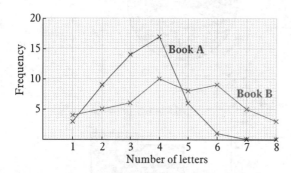

b There are more shorter words in A than in B. B has a greater range of the number of letters in words.

12 Averages

Levels 3–5 (p. 129)

1 a The mode is 18

b 15, 18, 18, 19, 21, 24

The median is

$$\frac{18 + 19}{2} = 18.5$$

c Total = 115
Mean = $115 \div 6 = 19.2$ (1 dp)

d Range = $24 - 15 = 9$

2 Chris' Cabs because the times are more consistent and more likely to be less than 16 mins.

Level 6 (p. 129)

3 a

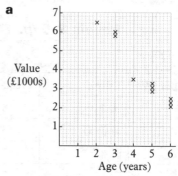

Age (years)

b Negative correlation.
As the age increases the value decreases.

Level 7 (p. 136)

1 a 5.5, 15.5, 25.5, 65.5
(these are in £1000s)

b

$$\frac{25 \times 5500 + 39 \times 15\,500 + 10 \times 25\,500 + 6 \times 35\,500}{25 + 39 + 10 + 6}$$

$$= \frac{1\,390\,000}{80} = £17\,375$$

c The modal group is 11–20

Level 8 (p. 136)

	Surgery	Clinic
a Median	20	22
b Lower quartile	14	13
c Upper quartile	27	32
d Interquartile range	13	19

e The waiting times at the surgery are generally shorter than those at the clinic. They are also more consistent in length of waiting times.

13 Probability

Levels 3–5 (p. 142)

1

b   c   a

0   0.5   1

2   **a**   red   **b** $\frac{3}{8}$ **c**   10
    d   2 blue counters

3   **a**   Method 2
    b   Method 1
    c   Method 3

Level 6 (p. 142)

4   **a**

		Dice				
		1	2	3	4	5	6
Coin	H	H, 1	H, 2	H, 3	H, 4	H, 5	H, 6
	T	T, 1	T, 2	T, 3	T, 4	T, 5	T, 6

    b $\frac{3}{12} = \frac{1}{4}$ **c** $1 - \frac{1}{4} = \frac{3}{4}$

Level 7 (p. 147)

1   **a**   100   **b** $\frac{8}{100} = \frac{2}{25}$
    c $\frac{35}{100} = \frac{7}{20}$ (or 0.35)
    d   By surveying more cars

Level 8 (p. 147)

2   **a** $\frac{2}{6} = \frac{1}{3}$
    b $\frac{1}{6} \times \frac{1}{2} = \frac{1}{12}$
    c $\frac{1}{6} \times \frac{1}{6} = \frac{1}{36}$

3   **a**

    b $0.6 \times 0.6 = 0.36$
    c $(0.6 \times 0.4) + (0.4 \times 0.6)$
       $= 0.24 + 0.24 = 0.48$

159

At appropriate stages the marks to be awarded are shown as (✓).

1 Whole numbers

Levels 3–5 (p. 9)

1 a 2345 (✓)   **b** 5432 (✓)   **c** 0 (✓)

2 a
$$\begin{array}{r} £13 \\ \times\ 25 \\ \hline 260 \\ 65 \\ \hline £325 \end{array}$$ (✓)
(✓)

25 CDs cost £325

b $18)\overline{3\ 0^{12}0}\ \underline{1\ 6}\ r12$ (✓ if remainder 12 shown)

16 packs of video tapes can be bought with £300 (✓)

3 a −3°C (✓)   **b**   **c** −2°C (✓)

8 °C →

Level 6 (p. 10)

4 a $-4-5=-9$ (✓)   **b** $-4--5=1$ (✓)

5 $T=\dfrac{4\times15}{-2}=\dfrac{60}{-2}=-30$ (✓)

Levels 5–7 (p. 14)

1 a $821-647=174$ (✓)
b $a\times b\times5=40$, where $a\times b=8$ (e.g. 2×4) (✓)
c $1400\div100=14$ (✓)
d $182\div7=26$ (✓)
e $a-b=31$ (e.g. $32-1$) (✓)
f $37\times9=333$ (✓)

2 a
$$\begin{array}{r} £27 \\ \times\ 34 \\ \hline 810 \\ 108 \\ \hline £918 \end{array}$$ (✓)
(✓)

34 candles sell for £918

b $12)\overline{2\ 0^{8}0}\ \underline{1\ 6}\ r8$ (✓ with remainder 8)

16 full boxes can be packed (✓)

3 $K=\dfrac{14.2\times37.4}{80.4-13.53}=\dfrac{531.08}{66.87}=7.941\,977$ (✓)

4   A $86\,850\,000\div347\,400=£250$
    B $119\,945\,000\div521\,500=£230$
    C $98\,784\,000\div403\,200=£245$
    D $170\,977\,500\div670\,500=£255$

    a Town B has the lowest tax per person (✓)
    b Town D has the highest tax per person (✓)

Level 8 (p. 15)

5 a 1.5×10^{10} (✓)
b $1.5\times10^{10}\times9.46\times10^{12}$ (✓) $=1.419\times10^{23}$ (✓)
6 $10^{600}\div10^{303}$ (✓) $=10^{600-303}=10^{297}$ (✓)

2 Fractions, decimals and percentages

Levels 3–5 (p. 22)

1 a $16\div2=8$ (✓)   **c** $16-a$ or $16-8=8$ (✓)
b $\frac{4}{16}=\frac14$ (✓)   **d** $16-4=12$ (✓)

2 To find the quantities needed for 9 people, first divide by 6 and then multiply by 9 (i.e. multiply by 1.5).
Garlic: $2\div6\times9=3$ cloves
Chick peas: $4\div6\times9=6$ ounces
Olive oil: $4\div6\times9=6$ tablespoons
Paste: $5\div6\times9=7\frac12$ (fluid ounces) (2✓)

3 a $\frac{9}{12}=\frac34$ (✓)
b $\frac34\times100=75\%$ (✓)
c $\frac23\times12=8$ shaded triangles (✓)

4 a $\frac{5}{100}\times30=£1.50$ (✓)
b $\frac25\times4=£1.60$ (✓)
c £1.50 (✓)

Level 6 (p. 23)

5 a Quantity of one 'part' of paint $=12\div3$
$=4$ litres (✓)
So $2\times4=8$ litres of red paint are needed. (✓)
b Total quantity of orange paint made
$=12+8=20$ litres (✓)

Levels 5–7 (p. 26)

1 a 0.36 (✓)   **b** 0.1 (✓)   **c** 0.08 (✓)

2 a $\frac12+\frac14+\frac18=\frac48+\frac28+\frac18=\frac78$
So fourth piece is $1-\frac78=\frac18$ of cake (✓)
b $\frac14=\frac{4}{16}$ (✓)
So weight of $\frac14$ of cake $=$ weight of $\frac{1}{16}\times4$
$=20\times4=80$ g (✓)

3 a Percentage of pupils in Year 9
$=\dfrac{(90+70)}{295}\times100=54.2\%$ (✓)
b Boys : girls $=150:145$ (✓)
$=150\div150:145\div150=1:0.967$ (✓)

4 a $1-\frac38=\frac88-\frac38=\frac58$ (✓)
b $\frac58\times100=62\frac12\%$ (✓)
c $\frac38\times24=£9$ (✓)

Level 8 (p. 27)

5 a Value of computer after 2 years
$=£800\times\dfrac{80}{100}\times\dfrac{80}{100}$ (✓) $=£512$ (✓)
b Value of computer when new
$=£704\times\dfrac{100}{80}\times\dfrac{100}{80}$ (✓) $=£1100$ (✓)
c i 0.8^2 or 0.64 (✓)   **ii** 0.8^n (✓)
d Value after 4 years $=£1500\times0.8^4$ (✓) $=£614.40$ (✓)
e $0.8^3=0.512\ (>\frac12)$, $0.8^4=0.4\ (<\frac12)$ (✓ for method)
So it will take 4 years for the value of any computer to fall by half its original value.

At appropriate stages the marks to be awarded are shown as ($\checkmark$).

3 Estimating

Levels 3–5 (p. 31)

1 350 000 or 346 000 ($\checkmark$)

2 **a** $x \div y = 5$ where $5 \times y = x$ ($\checkmark$)
    b $24 \div 3 + 1 = 9$ ($\checkmark$)

3 **a**

School	Number of pupils	To the nearest 100	To the nearest 10
Olney	884	900	880
Mesnes	662	700	660
Heaton	788	800	790
Pendle	906	900	910

(4$\checkmark$)

    b Any two numbers between 650 and 655 inclusive. (2$\checkmark$)

Level 6 (p. 31)

4 **a** $4667 \div 359 \ (=13)$ or $4667 \div 13 \ (=359)$ ($\checkmark$)
    b $1138 - 377 \ (=761)$ or $1138 - 761 \ (=377)$ ($\checkmark$)
    c $1830 - 1103 \ (=727)$ or $727 + 1103 \ (=1830)$ ($\checkmark$)
    d $17 \times 311 \ (=5287)$ or $5287 \div 311 \ (=17)$ ($\checkmark$)

Levels 5–7 (p. 34)

1 **a** Cost of 4 garden pots £2.45 $\times$ 4 = £9.80 ($\checkmark$)
    b $12 \div 2.45 = 4.89$
       So you can buy 4 pots with £12.00 ($\checkmark$)
    c $12 \div 4.49 = 2.67$
       So you can buy 2 pairs of pots with £12.00 ($\checkmark$)
    d £4.49 $\times$ 3 pairs + £2.45 $\times$ 1 single = £15.92
       So 7 pots is the greatest number you can buy with £16.00 ($\checkmark$)

2

Number	Rounded to 1 sf	Rounded to 2 sf	Rounded to 3 sf
0.5182	0.5	0.52	0.518
10.099	10	10	10.1
58.42	60	58	58.4
3486	3000	3500	3490

3 $\dfrac{81 \times 155}{42.4 \times 2.4} \approx \dfrac{80 \times 200}{40 \times 2}$ (1 sf) ($\checkmark$) = 200 ($\checkmark$)

Level 8 (p. 35)

4 **a** 5.115 ($\checkmark$)   **b** 5.1249 or 5.125 ($\checkmark$)

5 $\sqrt{\dfrac{12.2^3 \times 14.3}{440 \times 9.6^2}} \approx \sqrt{\dfrac{10^3 \times 10}{400 \times 10^2}}$ (1 sf) ($\checkmark$) = $\dfrac{1}{2}$ ($\checkmark$)

4 Patterns and sequences

Levels 3–5 (p. 39)

1 **a** Either 16×2 or 32×1 ($\checkmark$)
    b $32 \div 6$ does not go exactly; 6 is not a factor of 32 ($\checkmark$)

2 **a**

($\checkmark$)

    b $22 \div 2 \times 5 = 55$ ($\checkmark$)
    c Number of white tiles in odd pattern
       = ((Length + 1) $\div$ 2 $\times$ 5) − 2 or
       ((Length − 1) $\div$ 2 $\times$ 5) + 3 ($\checkmark$)

3 **a** 10, 15, 21 ($\checkmark$)
    b Two prime numbers (e.g. 2, 3, 11, 13, 17, 19, ...) ($\checkmark$)
    c 15 is not prime, it has 2 factors; 3 and 5 as well as 1 and 15 ($\checkmark$)

Level 6 (p. 40)

4 **a** 12 grey, 9 red ($\checkmark$)   **c** $T = 4N − 3$ ($\checkmark$)
    b 28 grey, 29 red ($\checkmark$)

Levels 5–7 (p. 43)

1 **a** 49 grey, 4 blue ($\checkmark$)
    b $14^2 = 196$ grey, 4 blue ($\checkmark$)
    c n^2 grey, 4 blue ($\checkmark$)
    d $n^2 + 4$ ($\checkmark$)
    e $n^2 + n^2 + 3$ ($\checkmark$) = $2n^2 + 3$ ($\checkmark$)

5 Formulas and equations

Levels 3–5 (p. 48)

1 **a** x^2 ($\checkmark$)   **c** $x \times 2, x + x$ ($\checkmark$)
    b $x \div 3$ ($\checkmark$)   **d** e.g. $4x, 2x + 2x$ ($\checkmark$)

2 **a** $2 \times n$ ($\checkmark$)   **b** $2n − 5$ ($\checkmark$)

3 **a** $n + n \ldots + n + n = 12n$ ($\checkmark$)
    b $12n = 60$ ($\checkmark$) so $n = 5$ ($\checkmark$)

Level 6 (p. 49)

4 **a** Sapna : $3m − 4$ ($\checkmark$) Dale : $2m + 1$ ($\checkmark$)
    b $3m − 4 = 2m + 1$ ($\checkmark$)
    c $3m − 4 = 2m + 1$
       $3m − 2m = 1 + 4$
       $m = 5$ ($\checkmark$)

5

x	y	
1	−1	too low
2	3	too high
1.5	0.75	too high (✓ for attempt between 1 and 2)
1.4	0.36	too high
1.3	−0.01	too low
1.35	0.1725	too high (✓ for attempt at 1.3 and 1.4)

The value which gives the solution nearest to 0 $x = 1.3$ (1 dp) ($\checkmark$)

Levels 5–7 (p. 54)

1 $x + y$; $8a$; $-5q$; $5x + 5y - 4w$; $-4k$; $4x^2$ (3✓)

2   **a**

24 °C →

   b $T < 24$ (✓)
   c $-9 \leqslant T < 12$ (✓)

3   **a** $P = \dfrac{x^2(x - 1)}{4}$

   $P = \dfrac{5^2(5 - 1)}{4} = \dfrac{25 \times 4}{4} = 25$ (✓)

   b $Q = \dfrac{5y^3}{6}$

   $Q = \dfrac{5 \times 3^3}{6} = \dfrac{5 \times 27}{6} = 22.5$ (✓)

4 $6x - 2 = 4x + 5$
   $6x - 4x = 5 + 2$
   $2x = 7$
   $x = 3.5$ (✓)
   Area of square $= (4x + 5)^2 = (4 \times 3.5 + 5)^2$
   $\qquad\qquad\qquad = 19^2 = 361 \text{ cm}^2$ (✓)
   or
   Area of square $= (6x - 2)^2 = (6 \times 3.5 - 2)^2$
   $\qquad\qquad\qquad = 19^2 = 361 \text{ cm}^2$

Level 8 (p. 55)

5   **a** $y \geqslant 2$ (✓) $x \leqslant 2$ (✓) $y \leqslant x + 1$ (✓)

   b

6   **a** $2(x - 3) - (x - 7) = 2x - 6 - x + 7$
   $\qquad\qquad\qquad\qquad = x + 1$ (✓)
   b $(x - 2)(x + 3) = x^2 + 3x - 2x - 6$
   $\qquad\qquad\qquad\quad = x^2 + x - 6$ (✓)
   c $(x + 5)^2 = x^2 + 5x + 5x + 25$
   $\qquad\qquad\quad = x^2 + 10x + 25$ (✓)

7   **a** $5 - 3x = 6x + 11$
   $-3x - 6x = 11 - 5$
   $\qquad -9x = 6$
   $\qquad\quad x = -\dfrac{6}{9} = -\dfrac{2}{3}$
   b $2(x - 1) = 6$
   $2x - 2 = 6$ (✓)
   $\qquad 2x = 8$
   $\qquad\; x = 4$ (✓)
   c $3x = 5(x - 1)$
   $3x = 5x - 5$
   $5 = 2x$
   $x = 2\frac{1}{2}$ (✓)

At appropriate stages the marks to be awarded are shown as (✓).

6   Functions and graphs

Levels 3–5 (p. 59)

1   **a**   A(2, 0), B(3, 1), C(4, 2)
   (2✓ *for all 3 correct*, ✓ *for 1 or 2 correct*)

   b   (11, 9) (✓)
   The x co-ordinate is one more than the triangle number.
   The y co-ordinate is one less than the triangle number. (✓)

   c   There needs to be a difference of two between the x and the y co-ordinates.
   $(x - y = 10 - 9 = 1 \neq 2)$ (✓)

2   **a**

(2✓)

   b   Square (✓)
   c   P′(0, 0), Q′(0, 6), R′(6, 6), S′(6, 0)

(2✓)

   d $36 \div 4 = 9$ times larger
   or (linear scale factor)$^2 = 3^2 = 9$ times larger (✓)

Level 6 (p. 60)

3   **a, b**

   c $y = nx$ (e.g. $y = -2x, y = x, y = \frac{1}{3}x$, etc.) (✓)
   d $y = x + 7$ (✓)

1 **a** $y = 3$ (✓), $x = 1$ (✓)

    b $y - x = 2$ is the equation of the line through D and B. (✓)

    c

      One of $y = 1$ or $y - x = 2$ or $y = -x$ (✓)

    d $2y + x = 22$ [1]
        $y - x = 2$ [2]
        $3y = 24$ [1] + [2]
        $y = 8$ (✓)

      Putting $y = 8$ in equation [2] gives
      $8 - x = 2$
        $x = 8 - 2 = 6$ (✓)

    e (6, 8) i.e. answers from part **d**

2 $8x + 6y = 10$ [1]
    $30x - 6y = 9$ [2] (✓ for rearrangement)
    $38x = 19$ ADD [1] + [2]
    $x = 0.5$ (✓)

    Putting $x = 0.5$ in equation [1] gives
    $4 + 6y = 10$
      $6y = 6$
       $y = 1$ (✓)

3 $x = 2$ (✓), $y = 1$ (✓)

4 $y = 2x^2 + 2$ (✓); $y = x^2$ (✓); $y = -2x^2$ (✓)

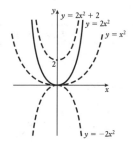

5 **i** acceleration/increasing speed (✓)

    ii level/same or constant speed (✓)

    iii constant deceleration/braking (✓)

7 2D and 3D shapes

1 **a, b** e.g.:

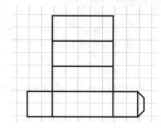

    (3✓ for net of cuboid, ✓ for flap)

2 **a** A (✓) **b** C (✓) **c** B, E (✓) **d** D (✓)
    e Pupil's drawing of angle between 90° and 180° (✓)

3 **a** N (✓) **b** S (✓)

4 **a** $a = 180° - 70° = 110°$ (✓)
        $b = 180° - 120° = 60°$ (✓)
        $c = 180° - 70° - b° = 180° - 70° - 60° = 50°$ (✓)

    b $d = 50°$ (alternate angles) (✓)
        $e = 140°$ (alternate angles) (✓)
        $f = 180° - 140° = 40°$ (angles on a straight line) (✓)
        Trapezium (✓)

1 C (✓)

2 **a** $x = 360° \div 6 = 60°$ **b** $y = 60° + 90° = 150°$

3 Using Pythagoras
    Base $= \sqrt{(13^2 - 5^2)}$ (✓)
         $= \sqrt{(169 - 25)} = \sqrt{144} = 12$ cm (✓)
    Area $= \frac{1}{2}$(base × height)
         $= \frac{1}{2}(12 \times 5) = 30$ cm^2 (✓)

4 **a** Using Pythagoras
      BC $= \sqrt{(450^2 + 350^2)}$ (✓) $= \sqrt{325\ 000} = 570$ m (✓)

    b To find the bearing, b,
        from B to C first find
        angle x.

      Using trigonometry
        $\tan x = \dfrac{350}{450} = 0.777\ ...$
         $x = \tan^{-1} 0.777\ ... = 37.9°$ (3 sf)
      Therefore $b = 90° - 37.9° = 52.1°$
      Bearing from B to C is 052.1° (✓)

c To find the bearing, c, from C to B first find angle y.
$y = 180 - 90 - 37.9 = 52.1°$ (angles in a triangle)
or $y = 52.1°$ (alternate angles)
Therefore $c = 180° + 52.1° = 232.1°$
Bearing from C to B = 232.1° (✓)

d $\cos 30 = \dfrac{450}{d}$ (✓)

$d = \dfrac{450}{\cos 30} = 520$

Distance from B to D
= 520 m (✓)

6 Correct size (×3) (✓)   Correct position (✓)

---

8   Position and movement

Levels 3–5 (p. 85)

1

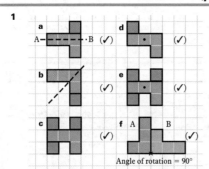

a A– – – –·B (✓)
b (✓)
c (✓)
d (✓)
e (✓)
f A   B (✓)
Angle of rotation = 90°

2

a (✓)   **b** (✓)   **c** (✓)

3

(2✓)

Level 6 (p. 86)

4 a 12 (✓)   **b** 2 (✓)
5 Circle drawn (✓)
Trapezium drawn (✓)
Square drawn (✓)

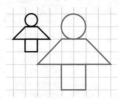

Levels 5–7 (p. 90)

1 a $42 \div 10 = 4.20$
$30 \div 7 = 4.29$
Scale factor = 4.20 (2 dp) (✓)
b $30 \div 10 = 3.00$
$21 \div 7 = 3.00$
Scale factor = 3.00 (2 dp) (✓)
c $21 \div 10 = 2.10$
$15 \div 7 = 2.14$
Scale factor = 2.10 (2 dp) (✓)

2

Scale 1 square : 1 m

(✓ for drawing rectangle 6 cm × 3 cm)
a Line 1.5 cm from side BC (✓)
b Line at 45° to side DC (✓)
c Shaded $\frac{1}{4}$ circle radius 1 cm, centre A (✓)

3

Scale 1 cm : 1 m

(4✓)

Level 8 (p. 91)

4 $\dfrac{h}{70} = \dfrac{84}{60}$ (✓)

So $h = \dfrac{84 \times 70}{60} = 98$ mm (✓)

or scale factor = $70 \div 60$ (✓)
so $h = 84 \times 70 \div 60$ (✓)

5 Triangles ADE and ABC are similar.

So $\dfrac{AE}{AC} = \dfrac{DE}{BC}$ (✓)

$AE = \dfrac{12 \times 8.5}{6} = 17$ m (✓)

$CE = AE - AC = 17 - 8.5 = 8.5$ m (✓)

At appropriate stages the marks to be awarded are shown as (✓).

9 Units of measurement

Levels 3–5 (p. 96)

1 a 10 : 20 (✓) **b** 09 : 45 (✓) **c** 35 minutes (✓)
d 07 : 30 or 08 : 15 or 09 : 00 (✓)
e 08 : 15 (✓)
f

(✓)

2 a 6.4 cm (✓) 64 mm (✓)
b 16 mm = 1.6 cm
Length of pencil = 5.3 − 1.6 = 3.7 cm (✓)

3 a 2.2 kg (✓)
b 600 g = 0.6 kg (✓)
Mass of cheese = 2.2 − 0.6 = 1.6 kg (✓)

Level 6 (p. 97)

4 a Value between 4.9 and 5.1 cm (✓)
b Value between 7.7 and 7.9 in (✓)

5 a 1 kg (✓)
b Value between 0.5 and 0.7 litres (✓)
c Value between 4 and 9 mm (✓)

Levels 5–7 (p. 100)

1 a 7.2 cm (✓)
b Value between 2.6 and 2.8 kg (✓)
c Value between 5.32 m and 5.34 m (✓)

2 a 12 st 10 lb (✓)
b 14 st 3 lb (✓)

3 a

Time (min)	1	6	10	15	25	30	50
Capacity (litres)	12	72	120	180	300	360	600

(2✓)

b $C = 12T$ (✓)

c $T = \dfrac{C}{12} = \dfrac{5000}{12} = 416.666 \ldots$ minutes
416.666 … minutes = 6 hours 57 minutes
(rounding to nearest minute)

4 a £550 = 154 000 pesetas
So £1.00 = $\dfrac{154\,000}{550}$ = 280 pesetas

b 4600 ÷ 280 = 16.429 (3 sf)
Cost of bag = £16.43

5 a 10 minutes (✓)
b Adam and Belinda passed each other going in opposite directions (✓)

c 50 minutes = $\dfrac{50}{60} = \dfrac{5}{6}$ hours

Average speed = $\dfrac{\text{Distance}}{\text{Time}}$

Average speed = $\dfrac{10}{\frac{5}{6}} = \dfrac{10 \times 6}{5}$ = 12 km/h (✓)

d Time Belinda was moving = 20 + 15 + 10
= 45 minutes = $\frac{3}{4}$ hours

Average speed = $\dfrac{10}{\frac{3}{4}} = \dfrac{10 \times 4}{3}$ = 13.3 km/h (✓)

e 10 and 20 minutes (✓)

10 Perimeter, area and volume

Levels 3–5 (p. 105)

1 a i Perimeter = 10 cm (✓) **ii** Area = 6 cm² (✓)
b i Perimeter = 18 cm (✓) **ii** Area = 8 cm² (✓)

2 a 7 (✓) **b** 10 (✓)

3 a Any shape (other than the one shown) with 6 tiles connected correctly. (✓)

4 a 5 × 3 = 15 cm² (✓)
b $\frac{1}{2}$ × 6 × 8 = 24 cm² (✓)
c $\frac{1}{2}$ × 4 × 7 = 14 cm² (✓)

5 a 12 × 2 = 24 (✓) **b** 6 + (12 × 2) = 30 (✓)

Level 6 (p. 106)

6 a Circumference = π × diameter
= π × 12 = 37.69 mm (✓)
Distance moved = 2 × circumference
= 2 × 37.69 = 75.4 mm (3 sf) (✓)

b Number of turns = $\dfrac{\text{Distance}}{\text{Circumference}}$

= $\dfrac{201}{\pi \times 16} = \dfrac{201}{50.27}$

= 3.998 = 3.40 (3 sf) (✓)

7 Length of side = $\sqrt{9}$ = 3
Perimeter = 3 × 4 = 12 cm (✓)

8 7 × 4 = 28 cm² (✓)

9 $\frac{h}{2}(7 + 5) = 24$
12h = 48, so h = 4 (✓)

Levels 5–7 (p. 110)

1 a Area of shaded face = $\frac{1}{2}$ × 7 × 8 (✓) = 28 m² (✓)
b Volume of prism = Area of base × Height
= 28 × 12 = 336 m³ (✓)

2 a Area of semicircle = $\frac{1}{2}\pi r^2 = \frac{1}{2}(\pi \times 5^2)$
= 39.27 cm² (2 dp) (✓)
b Perimeter of semicircle = $\frac{1}{2}\pi d + d$ = 15.708 + 10
= 25.71 cm (2 dp) (✓)

3 $\dfrac{h}{60} = \dfrac{20}{100}$ (✓) so $h = \dfrac{20 \times 60}{100}$ = 12 cm (✓)
or cross-section area = 100 ÷ 20 = 5 cm² (✓)
5h = 60 so h = 12 cm (✓)

4 If width is x cm, then length is 3x cm and perimeter is
3x + x + 3x + x = 8x cm
8x = 48 cm so x = 6 cm
Area of rectangle = x × 3x = 3x^2
= 3 × (6²) = 108 cm² (✓)

5 $36 \div 2 = 18, 100 \div 2 = 50, 50 \div 2 = 25$ (✓)
Number of cubes that will fit in box $= 18 \times 50 \times 25$
$= 22\,500$ (✓)

6 Area of shaded region $= \pi(3^2) - \pi(1.2^2)$ (✓)
$= 28.27 - 4.52 = 23.75$ (2 dp) (✓)

7 Surface area of prism $= (\frac{1}{2} \times 5 \times 12) + (\frac{1}{2} \times 5 \times 12)$
$+ (13 \times 10) + (12 \times 10) + (5 \times 10) = 360\,cm^2$ (✓)

Level 8 (p. 111)

8 Surface area of curved face $= \frac{1}{2}(4\pi r^2) = 2\pi r^2$ (✓)
Surface area of face $= \pi r^2$ (✓)
Surface area of hemisphere $= 2\pi r^2 + \pi r^2 = 3\pi r^2$
$= 3\pi 4^2 = 48\pi$
$= 150.8\,cm^2$ (4 sf) (✓)

9

$4\pi r^2$	lbh	$\frac{1}{2}bh$	$\frac{4}{3}\pi r^3$	$4(r+b)$	$\dfrac{\pi h^2}{b}$	
			✓	✓		Length
✓		✓				Area
		✓		✓		Volume

(2✓)

At appropriate stages the marks to be awarded are shown as (✓).

11 Units of measurement

Levels 3–5 (p. 119)

1 a Monday 28 (✓) Tuesday 22 (✓) Wednesday 15 (✓)
b Thursday: $2\frac{1}{4}$ discs (✓) Friday: 6 discs (✓)
c Thursday (✓)
d The pictogram summarises the data and shows it in such a way that it is easily understood. Makes it easy to compare the figures. (✓)
e A tally chart is easy to add to, and to use to collect the data. (✓)

2 a Number of programmes recorded
$= 16 + 11 + 12 + 13 = 52$ (✓)
b Number of films recorded $= 16 + 12 = 28$ (✓)
c

	Channel 1	Channel 3
Soaps	7	10
Comedy	4	6

(2✓)

3 a Dog (✓) **b** Fish and mice (✓)
c Number of cats $= 40 \times \frac{1}{4} = 10$ (✓)
d Number of dogs = number between 12 and 15 (✓)

Level 6 (p. 120)

4 a There are too many tallies. The tallies needed to be counted up to make the chart clearer. (✓)
b 180 (✓)
c A pie chart will show better a comparison between the holiday choices, as a fraction of those questioned. It is not how many who have made a choice that is important, but the proportion of each that have shown a preference. (✓)

d Ski 26°, Winter abroad 70°, Summer sun 174°, Touring 44°, UK holiday 46°
(*2 angles correct* ✓; *all angles correct* 2✓; *labels and title* ✓)

Holiday preferences

Levels 5–7 (p. 124)

1 a Between 30% and 40% (✓)
b Between 15 and 25 (✓)
c There are many more items included in B than A (✓)
d (*2 angles correct* ✓; *all angles correct* 2✓; *labels and title* ✓)

Snack bar C: 200 items

2 a Any three from:
Amounts overlap
No 'don't know' box
Amounts are too small
Groupings need to be bigger to cover more amounts (3✓)
b Need to include both girls and boys, and pupils of different ages/year, groups and backgrounds. (2✓)

3 a There is little change in Gary's figures. Therefore his week 11 sales are likely to be similar to his sales in weeks 1–10.
b Though Ali's sales figures in some weeks are higher than Gary's, in many more weeks they are lower than Gary's. Therefore, Ali's overall sales are lower.

12 Averages

Levels 3–5 (p. 130)

1 a Mode $= 2$ (✓)
b Range $= 6 - 1 = 5$ (✓)
c Median $= 3$ (✓)
d Mean $= 33 \div 10 = 3.3$ (✓)

2 To score an average of 12, Jerry must score $3 \times 12 = 36$ over three games. In 2 games he has scored $8 + 15 = 23$ points. So he must score $36 - 23 = 13$ points in his final game.

3 a Mean $= \dfrac{\text{Total number of pets}}{\text{Total number of pupils}}$

$= \dfrac{(5 \times 0) + (3 \times 1) + (2 \times 2) + (2 \times 3) + (3 \times 4) + (2 \times 5)}{5 + 3 + 2 + 2 + 3 + 2}$ (✓)

$= \dfrac{35}{17} = 2.06$ (3 sf) (✓)

b Modal number $= 0$ pets (✓)
c Median number is 9th value $= 2$ pets (✓)

Level 6 (p. 131)

4 a Mean number of errors = $\dfrac{\text{Total number of errors}}{\text{Total number of pupils}}$

$= \dfrac{(1 \times 5) + (2 \times 6) + (3 \times 7) + (4 \times 5) + (5 \times 3)}{5 + 6 + 7 + 5 + 3}$ (✓)

$= \dfrac{73}{26} = 2.81$ (3 sf) (✓)

b Median = 13th value = 3 errors (✓)

c The mean, as it is the result of a calculation, need not be one of the given number of errors. The median is a given number of errors. (✓)

5 a As the temperature rises, the number of cups of hot soup decreases (inverse proportion, negative correlation). (✓)

b No relation (no correlation). (✓)

Levels 5–7 (p. 137)

1 a As the number of hours of clear sky increases, the temperature decreases (inverse proportion, negative correlation). (✓)

b Line of best fit drawn ±2 mm (✓)
2 °C → 4.8 h ± 1 h (✓)
4 h → 3 °C ± 1 °C (✓)

(graph: Hours of clear sky vs Temperature (°C))

2 a Mean = $\dfrac{\sum fx}{\sum f}$

$\sum fx = (34.5 \times 3) + (44.5 \times 8) + (54.5 \times 11) + (64.5 \times 9)$
$+ (74.5 \times 13) + (84.5 \times 6) = 3115$ (✓)

Mean = $\dfrac{3115}{50} = 62.3$ paces (✓)

b Median is 25th → group 60–69 (✓)

Level 8 (p. 139)

3 a Median age = 47 ± 2 (✓)

b Interquartile range: 150 on vertical axis → 57 ± 2
50 on vertical axis → 36 ± 2
Interquartile range = 57 − 36 = 21 (2 ✓)

c Percentage of population under 50 ≈ $\dfrac{116}{200} \times 100$

$= 58\% \pm 2\%$ (✓)

13 Probability

Levels 3–5 (p. 143)

1 a $\frac{2}{5}$ (✓) **b** 0 (✓)

c Probability of getting a blue or brown cube is $\frac{2}{5} = 0.4$

(number line with X marked) (✓)

d Probability of **not** getting a green cube is $1 - \frac{1}{5} = \frac{4}{5} = 0.8$

(number line with X marked) (✓)

2 a Probability of red = $\frac{3}{8}$
Probability of green = $\frac{3}{8}$
So red is no more likely than green. (✓)

b The wheel is just as likely to stop on yellow the second time as it was the first.
So probability of yellow = $\frac{1}{8}$ (✓)

c

All segments one colour. (✓)

d

Any four segments one colour. Remaining four segments a second colour. (✓)

3 a Coin is just as likely to land on heads the fifth time as it was the other four times. So probability of heads = $\frac{1}{2} = 0.5$

(number line with X marked)

b Probability of 2 heads = $\frac{1}{2} \times \frac{1}{2} = \frac{1}{4}$ (✓)

c Probability of not throwing 2 tails
$= 1 -$ probability of 2 tails $= 1 - \frac{1}{4} = \frac{3}{4}$ (✓)

Level 6 (p. 144)

4 a It is possible that the bag contains many different coloured counters and that it is only by chance that she has picked only red counters. (✓)

b The probabilities of picking counters from the bag depend on the colours of the counters in the bag, not on the colours of the counters already taken out of the bag. (✓)

Levels 5–7 (p. 148)

1 a

+	2	4	6	8
1	3	5	7	9
3	5	7	9	11
5	7	9	11	13
7	9	11	13	15

(✓)

b Probability that answer is greater than 9 $= \frac{6}{16} = \frac{3}{8}$ (✓)

c Probability that answer is a square number
= Probability that answer is 9 $= \frac{4}{16} = \frac{1}{4}$ (✓)

d Probability that answer is an even number = 0 (✓)

2 a Estimated probability of red $= \frac{30}{60} = \frac{1}{2}$ (✓)

b 10 times (✓)

c Probability only tells you what is likely to happen, not what actually happens. (✓)

d To improve the accuracy of his results, Tony needs to do more trials, i.e. throw the cube more times. (✓)

Level 8 (p. 149)

3 a Events are independent. So probability of passing through both sets of lights without having to stop = 0.3 × 0.3 = 0.09 (✓)

b Probability of being stopped at only one set of lights = (0.7 × 0.3) + (0.3 × 0.7) (✓)
= 0.21 + 0.21 = 0.42 (✓)

c Probability of being stopped at first set of lights = 0.7
Number of times Karen can expect to be stopped in 80 journeys = 0.7 × 80 = 56 times

In the days before the tests

- Read through the 'What you need to know?' sections for your tier again.

- Read the Test Yourself tests and the Practice Questions for your tier of entry. Check the answers too and make sure that you know how to do all of the questions you have seen.

- Ask your teacher for copies of the Maths Tests from last year and the year before. If you try questions from these papers, ask your teacher for the answers and check your work.

On the day of the tests

Take the right equipment with you: pen, pencil, rubber, ruler, protractor or angle measurer, compasses and a calculator for the calculator paper and anything else that your teacher has told you to bring.

In the examination room

- Read each question carefully. Make sure you understand what the question is about and what you are expected to do.

- In all questions show any working out you do, even if you are using a calculator. You may lose marks if you do not show working.

- When using rulers, protractors or compasses make sure you use them accurately.

- The number of marks for each question is always shown on the paper.

- Give your answers to an appropriate degree of accuracy. **Do not** make them inaccurate by rounding off.

- Always round money answers to the nearest penny and to a given number of significant figures **where this is asked for**.

- If you find a question too hard, go on to the next question. But try to write something for each part of every question.

- If you have spare time at the end, use it wisely to check over your answers and working.

Acknowledgements

The publishers thank the following for permission to reproduce copyright material: Leslie Garland Picture Library 80; Collections/Brian Shuel 68; Martyn Chillmaid 112, 145, 147.

Many thanks to the Key Maths authors for their contributions to this text and in particular to David Baker who inspired some of the introductions to the chapters.

Thanks to Graham Newman, Chief Examiner in Mathematics for Key Stage 3, for the Practice Examination Questions and Test Tips and for his invaluable contributions at review.

Thanks to the team at Stanley Thornes, in particular Adrian Wheaton, Malcolm Tomlin and Lorna Godson.

First published 1999 by
Stanley Thornes (Publishers) Ltd, Ellenborough House, Wellington Street, CHELTENHAM GL50 1YW

ISBN 0 7487 4453 3

00 01 02 03/10 9 8 7 6 5 4 3   Printed and bound in Spain by Mateu Cromo

Typeset by Tech Set Ltd, Gateshead